D1547376

The Lost Art
of Church
Fund Raising

The Lost Art
of Church
Fund Raising

Ashley Hale

Precept Press, Inc., Chicago

96   95   94   93   92   5   4   3   2   1

Library of Congress Catalog Card Number:

International Standard Book Number:

Precept Press, Inc.
160 East Illinois Street
Chicago, Illinois 60611

Composition by Point West, Inc., Carol Stream IL

Printed in the United States of America

The material in Part One of this book is adapted from articles and columns by Mr. Hale that originally appeared in *The Clergy Journal*, PO Box 162527, Austin, TX, 78716. This copyrighted material is used here with the permission of that magazine.

Contents

Contents (Continued)

1

A FAREWELL TO ALMS

I SPENT MOST OF World War II in India as a guest of the
United States Army Air force together with three thousand other guests. I got one of the Indian civilians on our
base to explain Indian currency to me.

The largest coin, the rupee, was then about 25 cents.
The next-largest, the anna, about a tenth of that. The next
to that, about a twentieth of that... "Whoa! I cried. That
little coin—what good is it? What can you use that for?"

My tutor shrugged. "Give it to the poor."

What had started in a lesson in currency had become a lesson in almsgiving.

This little collection of articles about church fund raising concerns giving about the alms-giving level. I would like to believe that this book will ignite a flame that will revolutionize church fund raising. Well, we know the new methods. Now all we have to do is use them.

WHAT I AM ALL ABOUT

THE CHURCHES OF NORTH America are spinning around, wanting to go forward but actually going nowhere.

Like all organizations with a long history (and they have the longest) they are having difficulty adapting once venerated goals, philosophy, and methods to the rapidly-changing circumstances of the present age.

Financially, the churches are falling behind every year—not dramatically at any one point but surely, slowly, falling behind. Once the largest givers on the planet they have been giving to others about 20 percent of their income—not much, when weighed against their preaching and teaching about giving historically.

The United States, Canadian churches, and others have been pushed out of their historic roles so far as giving is concerned. They have been so involved and committed to their own existence that they are hard pressed to retain their historic roles as philanthropists.

The churches are in a trap. Preaching generosity, they are exhibiting that they don't really believe in it because they are not practicing it themselves. The financial needs of the church take first place but they teach and preach to their members to do the opposite. The church budget takes first place. What is needed is for the churches to break out of their chains and set their members a good example.

To achieve this they need radically improved attitudes toward and methods of fund raising.

That is what I am all about.

3

THE VANISHING CHURCH MORTGAGE

For most churches, giving from capital is largely terra incognita.

THE CHURCH MORTGAGE IS as traditional as apple pie, baseball, and the 4th of July. But today at least 75 percent of all church mortgages are unnecessary. Fund raising technique has improved.

True, very young churches often, but not always, must build new facilities that they cannot yet pay for. True, churches relocating that cannot advantageously sell their old property often, but not always, must move into new buildings before they are paid for. But most mortgages are incurred by neither new nor relocating churches; they are incurred by churches that could raise the money instead of borrowing it.

Yet many a church has paid, in principle and interest, for a new building twice—or even three times—over. Paying for a new building out of the budget is the slowest and most expensive way a church can go.

The amount of money that a congregation will give to a building-fund campaign is almost always under-estimated. But the record is clear: in competently-managed campaigns for maximum goals, 85 percent of American and Canadian churches can raise as much for a building fund in three years as the members will give to the annual operating budget for the same period. About 15 percent of the churches can raise twice that much.

The church saddled with a mortgage that tries to make significant, vigorous forward movement is likely to experience the ultimate in congregational frustration. It's like running the 220 high hurdles carrying an 80-pound knapsack. The conservative members of the Board—and even of the congregation—will always vote against a proposal for a new venture that involves increased expenditure: "...until we pay off the mortgage," even though the mortgage may be for 20 or 30 years.

Adding a big debt-service item to the budget seldom generates a commensurate increase in the members' giving. Paying for debt retirement is a cheerless sort of thing. It has no "power to stir men's souls." (Or women's either, for that matter.) We have a term for what happens because a capital-fund item crowds its way into an operations budget: "program deficits." Something has to give, and debt-payments can't.

A tragedy is that creating capital funds from budget giving misses out on a great financial power: gifts *from* capital. Many secular nonprofit organizations receive more in gifts from their donors' capital than from their income. More members than we know give modestly to their churches' budgets from income and magnificently to their colleges or medical centers from capital. Of the 20 or 30 largest gifts to anything every year, only one or two are made to any religious organization. For the churches, the subject of gifts from capital is largely unexplored territory.

The 10 percent of your financially most-capable families —those who have capital, instead of mortgages on their own homes—will normally give 15 percent to 25 percent of your budget, but they can give 25 percent to 50 percent of your building fund—sometimes more. Yet, if you incorporate your building fund into the budget, they are unlikely to give more than 25 percent.

Every Christian family ought, at least once in its lifetime, to help build a church. Every generation ought to be a building generation—for itself or for others. But young families with big mortgages on their own homes, and with children in college, cannot double or triple their budget giving just because the budget includes a debt-retirement item. They have their own debt-retirement problems.

The spiritual impact of good giving—of great giving—is a phenomenon observed by all experienced church leaders. The impact is in direct relation to the size—the generosity—of the gift. The impact of giving an additional $5 a week to the budget is not likely to change many families' religious life importantly. But a big building-fund gift can have a significant impact, and give a real sense of being a church builder.

Another positive effect of a building-fund campaign as contrasted with a mortgage is not always experienced by *every* church that conducts a campaign, but it should be. Budget giving should *jump* at the end of the building-fund pledge-payment period. Most church families, after two or three years of paying on two pledges, are quite willing to consider increasing their budget giving, often dramatically. Of course, they do have to be asked, and many churches forget to ask.

Moral: Raise all that you can and only then think about borrowing.

WINNERS AND LOSERS

**Good fund raising and stewardship development
ought to promote each other.**

I CAN THINK OF no area of church work in which the gap
between the common and best methods is so wide as in
fund raising. Despite mountains of evidence to the con-
trary, most churches persist in staying with methods that
have been long disproved—and they stay in genteel poverty. For this reason, most churches in the chart that fol-
lows fall into the loser column. But they need not.

ELEMENT	LOSERS	WINNERS
STYLE	promotion	organization
APPEAL	emotion	rational
FOCUS	the church's need to receive	the members' need to give
MOTIVE FOR GIVING	duty, compliance, repaying God	the gospel of good giving
GOAL	as low as possible	as high as possible
OBJECTIVE	to secure gifts	to make givers
QUANTITIVE EMPHASIS	the number of gifts	the size of gifts
PREPARATION	hasty	thorough
ADMINISTRATION	casual	professional
MANAGEMENT	none	professional
LEADERSHIP CRITERIA	popularity and willingness	size of gift or pledge
TERM OF CAMPAIGN	one or several days	several weeks
SOLICITATION	impersonal	personalized
GUIDANCE FOR THE INDIVIDUAL GIVER	rhetorical	individual
ROLE OF PASTOR	preacher and Mr. Fixit	interpreter and counselor
POST-CAMPAIGN	nothing	organized follow-up
PREDICTABLE RESULTS	uncertain, equivocal, fleeting	certain, unequivocal, enduring

Basically, there are only two criteria in predicting what a church will do in a major fund raising program. The first is the level of stewardship understanding and performance that the church has already achieved. For instance, no family ever joined the Seventh-day Adventists or Free Methodist Church and then found, to its horror, that it was expected to tithe. This is such a basic factor that in our estimating the capital fund-raising potential of a church, we work on the basis of "times the budget;" that is, how many times the current giving to the budget it can raise.

But there is another, at least equally operative factor: the extent to which the church will learn and apply what is now known about the elements of success, as contrasted with traditional but often groundless wisdom about fund-raising methods.

It has taken me 15 years to develop the table herewith. It is not entirely complete, but it contains all the major factors. Each line on this table is provable, based upon computerized analyses of more than 5,000 campaigns. To coin an old phrase, ignore it at your peril.

"But what," you may ask, "about not just fund raising but also stewardship development?" Well, the two lists of winners and losers would remain about the same. The trouble with most stewardship programs is that they are less specific about what you *do* than what you say.

Good fund raising and stewardship development ought to promote each other. A program for either that does not advance the cause of the other ought to be examined— there is probably something wrong. Check yourself out.

5

GETTING FIRST CHOICE LEADERS

When you tell a person that he or she is best qualified to be the leader, make sure that you are right.

Y OU SHOULD NEVER BE refused by a first-choice leader and you need not be. Individual circumstances are of infinite variety, but there are a few principles that, wisely applied, will assure your success. In enlisting a fund-raising General Chair, take three steps.

1. Select the best-qualified person.

2. Tell him (increasingly "her") that he is.

3. Assure him or her of your support and present evidence that other essential support is assured.

Usually the best way to do this is to gather a few friends

who either are, or know well, the financially most successful members. Decide who is best qualified for the job.

That is all: the best qualified to make the largest gift, to secure a few of the next-largest and enlist these other members at the top of the batting order, to bring them into the other top campaign positions, and to otherwise lead the enterprise.

Now, just go and tell him that he is the best-qualified. I don't, anywhere in this chapter, mean that you should do everything yourself. You and your friends ("selecting," above) can decide who does what.

Certain preparations must be made. Any intelligent person must have certain assurances. You may not be able to give all of them but be prepared as best you can. Some of them are:

- Your personal support.
- Official Board support. This is best-established by a resolution stating that the undersigned members of the Board will accept any position in the fund-raising organization that you and the General Chair ask them to take.
- The feasibility study report. (What, you did not have one? Shame!)
- The campaign plan, hopefully written by a pro.
- General Chair's manual.
- Campaign expense budget.
- Information about your consultant or campaign manager.
- Report on the congregational meeting authorizing the campaign.

Once the prospective top of the batting order objected, saying, "Eight or ten years ago I accepted a similar position for the annual member canvass and you guys left me all alone out there in left field." We showed him the organization chart in the campaign plan with the names of those Chairs already written in—subject to his taking the number one spot on the batting order. One more harrumph! and he said, "OK."

Two parting admonitions. When you (or any spokesman on the issue) tell a person that he is best-qualified, make sure that you are right. "Best-qualified" doesn't mean most willing, or most popular, or most experienced in church work. Whether presently or formerly active in church work has nothing to do with the matter. Try this test: will announcement of his acceptance send tremors throughout the congregation: "Gee whiz, they must really mean business this time."

Never, never, minimize the job. He (remember, increasingly "she") will certainly ask. "How much time will it take?" There is one, and only one, honest answer to that question: "It depends on who takes the job." That answer is honest because the truly capable executive delegates everything except what only he can do. How long does it take to lead a national campaign for an eight- or nine-figure goal?

I have recently collected what the nominee for the top of the batting order said when asked—his first words: "Let's see who I should have for my committee." "Do I have to make speeches?" [No]. "OK."

Batter up!

6

NEVER HEAR THE DEADLY "NO"

When your first choice says 'no' and asks 'who is your second choice?,' respond 'We have none. We assumed your acceptance.' Then, you'd better be telling the truth!

H OW OFTEN HAVE I heard, "We can't get them to help us." Now, don't you ever, *ever* descend to that plaintive, self-incriminating wail. Very, very rarely will any church member, no matter heretofore uninvolved, refuse when asked correctly to assume a responsibility that is right for that person.

If you have been reading any of my articles or columns, you know that the church should never, *never* beg for money. Now, listen up! You should never beg for time or talents, either. Nor need you.

There are five steps in securing a member for a particular important responsibility. Omit or violate any one of them, and you are in danger of hearing the deadly "no." Follow them—go to that much trouble—and you will forget that you ever heard a "no."

I learned these steps over a lifetime of securing only the best-qualified members for positions of top leadership in fund raising campaigns. But they are universals; they hold for any kind of volunteer church work.

1. Define the job. In the secular world, it is unthinkable to ask a person to take an undefined or ill-defined job. You must be able clearly to state the purpose, goal, standards of performance, and the ultimate benefits that will ensue from a successful enterprise.

2. Make it ad hoc. A cautious person might want to know not only how to get into, but also how to get out of, the proffered job. A definite accomplishment or time limit is a big help in enlisting hesitant or fearful persons.

3. Provide support. The prospective lay leader seldom wants to be left all alone out in left field. Tell who else is already, or will be, committed and involved.

When you ask, have along with you the person who has already accepted a related and superior position. If you are asking a person to accept the top leadership position, have the right member of your Board along and, preferably, the resolution of the Board asking that person to serve and assuring him or her of their individual and collective support.

Never ask a person to do for the church what that person hires other people to do in his or her own business, profession, or vocation. Do not ask a person to step down, in terms of authority or responsibility, from a secular-world position to a lower church position.

4. Select the best-qualified person. This rule must not be compromised. Do not take into consideration the person's probable willingness to accept—in other words, don't make it easy on yourself. Do not wear out your willing leaders; create new lay leaders. Given two equally qualified persons, go for the peripheral member every time.

5. Say, "You are the best-qualified." Do not ask the person to serve. Better that you should anoint him, tapping his shoulder with Excalibur and say, "Arise, Sir Chair." Be prepared to offer evidence that the Board or committee has examined the prospects thoroughly, and that he or she is the winner.

Never have an alternative in case the first-choice person refuses. You must be able to look him/her straight in the eye when asked, "Who is your second choice?" and say, "We have none. We have assumed your acceptance." And you had better be telling the truth.

Added to these five principles are two admonitions. As the pastor, you should seldom be the principal person to ask. You should support another lay- or project-leader who has already accepted. Use the key top leader building the committee or organization—with your advice, guidance, and assistance. But especially remember that if the person is to say "No," let him say it to a lay leader, not to you. Even so, you must make your desire for acceptance perfectly clear.

Also, the procedure here described is for enlisting a key chair or leader. Below that level, it is sometimes best to enlist at meetings. The key there is not to ask who will accept but simply put them to work. Very few will decline.

There is a vast pool of untapped lay leadership in your church. Most members have never been asked. Few have been asked correctly. A young pastor and I had lunch with the best-qualified member to lead a big campaign. The pastor knew that the man would not take the job but I was insistent that he be asked. "You know, if you had not asked me my feelings would have been hurt," he said.

7

FIVE WHO SAID YES

The reason that many of the financial elite have little or no record of church-work service is that they have not been asked.

I HAVE ALWAYS STRESSED the importance of securing your financially heaviest hitters for leadership of a major fund-raising program; the most generous but less wealthy givers have their place, but it is not at the top of the fund-raising organization. I have also suggested that the reason that many of the financial elite have little or no record of church-work service is that they have not been askcd.

Let's consider some first-choice campaign leaders and what they have said when asked to serve. In four of these cases I had a difficult time persuading the minister or Board to ask the first-choice person first.

Suin' Sam was a hard-boiled trial lawyer who intimidated almost everybody but he was obviously the best-qualified for what in those delicate days we called the Big Gifts division. The Campaign Chair, minister, and I went over and told him so. Sam just frowned. The minister turned to us and said, "I told you fellows he wouldn't. . ." Sam coughed, took out a pencil and pad of paper and asked, "Who should I have for my committee?" We tried not to gasp. Sam had been in church perhaps three times within the past two years.

About six months later I was in town and caught evening service. It was Laymen's Sunday and there was Sam in the pulpit. Afterward, I went up and said, "Sam, looks like you're back in church." "Sure," he said. "I have to come around and see how they're spending my money."

Wilbur was one of the most respected men in town, both as a banker and as a civic leader. When we asked him to head his church's big building fund campaign we trembled because he had been in Europe and therefore missed all the meetings of the campaign planning committee. As we made the usual remarks preparing to asking him; one of the men blurted out nervously, "Wilbur, these fellows want you for Campaign Chair." I died.

Wilbur looked almost unkindly at that fellow and said, "I have always done whatever my church asked me to do."

Jim was the obvious first choice and we made it clear that he was the best-qualified person in this large congregation to lead this big campaign. The best that we could get out of him was that he had promised his wife that he would ease off—as head of a major investment firm—and that they would take a trip around the world. He would accept the position only with his wife's consent. They would talk it over.

The next day he accepted. Asked how he did it he told us that he said, "But darling, I am the best qualified." He was great, but so was she. In a sense, she made the first gift.

In an Episcopal church in a wealthy suburb, it was difficult to select the Campaign Chair. The rector was hesitant to agree on the selection, but the Vestry and I persisted. The young rector said OK, but I will have to ask him to serve. So he and I had lunch with the leading candidate. Half-way through the lunch, he said "yes." The rector excused himself and the lay leader and I looked at each other. I said, "He was afraid that you would say no."

Easily the judge was first choice for Campaign Chair. But for years he had only slipped into early service; nobody knew what his interest in the church, much less the campaign, might be. He did accept and a few of us (as usual) were sitting around after the victory report meeting congratulating each other. Somebody said, "Judge, we never thought you would accept the leadership." The judge got a sort of dreamy look in his eyes and told us, "About two years ago I had a subjective religious experience, and I swore then that I would do anything that my church asked me to do. But I hadn't done anything for the church since."

We were embarrassed because we knew why. The judge did not have to tell us. He had not been asked.

8

STRATEGIC PLANNING

How you plan is more important than what you plan.

IN THE LAST FEW years before retiring, I guided at least a hundred churches through what we call the Congregational Development Program. The original purpose was to increase budget pledging radically. To do this, we had to have stronger goals. A very few of the participating churches doubled their pledging. The average gain was 3 percent.

The first activity for everybody was the preparation of a planning report for mid-range goals—neither long-range (ten years) nor short-range (one).

I did not commence this program innocent of how to plan the development of a church. But I learned more about planning therein than I had learned before or have since.

1. *How* you plan is more important than *what* you plan. Previously, I had started, and even ended, with either an ad hoc committee or a planning retreat of the Governing Board. But in the CDP, or "The Program" as we called it, the Plans Board consisted of three to five committees (never more nor less). The Chair of the committees plus the pastor and the Chair of the whole project constitute an inner circle with ultimate responsibility for developing a plan. Assuming an average of five members of a committee, that gives us initial involvement of 15 to 25 persons. (Hale's law #46: the larger the committee the less thinking gets done.) The Plans Board prepares the planning document report.

The committees always include membership (development and participation), services to the congregation, services to others, and financial. The financial committee price-tags the reports of the other committees of the Plans Board. Forbid the other committees to price anything lest somebody comes up with the cold-water treatment: "We can't afford it." This is not the church's standing finance committee. One or two others can be added if really (but not often) necessary. For example, facilities or endowment.

2. The first paragraph or page of each committee's report is a summary of their report, with all documentation to follow.

3. The Plans Board report on the other hand consists of its own report up front, followed by the three or five committees reports, followed by documentation.

4. The Plans Board takes their proposed planning report to the Governing Board and requests permission to take it to the congregation, with or without corrections. (Usually with.) *Important:* the Governing Board approves the draft

report only for congregational discussion—not for approval. But there might be some things in the draft report that the Governing Board does not want taken to the congregation, even on a draft basis. Hence the Board gets first crack at it.

5. The Plans Board conducts small home-meetings for consideration and discussion. Three persons at each meeting have distinct responsibilities: (a) the host, in whose home the meeting takes place. He or she selects the invitees, issues the invitations, and is in charge of the meeting as a social event; (b) the presenter and discussion leader, who should be a member of the Plans Board; and (c) the recorder, who takes notes, especially of suggested changes in the draft report. (No votes are taken, but the presenter and recorder should be sensitive to consensus, like our friends, the Friends.)

6. The report is re-drafted and submitted to the Governing Board for approval (this time).

7. The Governing Board approves and authorizes a campaign for operating fund pledges and/or calls for a denominational meeting to approve the planning report if denominational policy requires it.

8. The Plans Board report is reviewed every two or three years (one or the other, always the same periodicity.)

Within the general guidelines herein, your church should draw up a resolution stating the plan for conducting its own strategic planning operation. Don't take any other church's—or even your denomination's advice—if you can get away with that.

Suffuse the whole operation but accept no formal position on any of the committees or the Plans Board itself. Instead of having to sell your visions for the church that is to be, you will find the Plans Board anxious to hear them. Very anxious. All hearing aids volume will be turned up.

9

PLANNING THAT WORKS

Beware the two mistakes of planning extremes: asking the congregation to do either all the thinking or none.

L IVES THERE THE PASTOR with soul so dead, who never has said, "We're going to *plan* this church?" But the process of church development planning isn't necessarily popular, easy, or automatically productive. I suggest seven imperatives that, within my experience, make for planning that works.

1. THE PLANNERS. They should be respected, influential members. They are organized into an ad hoc Plans Council. Staff can plan all they want, but in so doing they can plan only their own performance. And no standing committee can plan the future of your church.

2. COMMITTEES OF THE PLAN COUNCIL. The Council will decide, but not investigate, research, or get down to the nitty-gritty. That is for the committees of the Council. You will need three: (A) services to ourselves; (B) services to others; and (C) finance. (You need "finance" because the other committees are not allowed to price their recommendations.) You might have another committee or two if you need them, but not more.

3. PRIORITIES. The Plans Council should recognize only three levels of priority: (A) what we *must* do; (B) what we *should* do, and (C) what we *could* do. No legitimate important recommendation should be rejected because it costs too much. But it can be given a "could do" priority.

4. FIRST DRAFT REPORT. When the committees have written their reports to the Council, and the Council its report to the Board, get a big rubber stamp and mark the reports "DRAFT." Present the plan to the Board for review and possible alteration, but not for formal acceptance.

5. GRASS ROOTS REVIEW. Now take the *draft* plan to the members for review, discussion, and ideas. This must not be just for effect, it must be legitimate. The Council has spoken, now it must listen. The best way to do this is through small meetings in the home. One person should record the major ideas, disagreements, and consensus on main issues.

6. SECOND DRAFT REPORT. When the Council has the feed-back from the home meetings, prepare a revised report, showing them the changes. Present this to the Board. The council is now through.

7. FUND RAISING. Now conduct whatever fund raising is indicated in support of the plan.

But don't let the plan become moribund. Any plan is obsolete before it gets off the drawing board. Revise the plan periodically; update it in the light of changes, circumstances and new accomplishments. I prefer frequent reviews but use whatever periodicity you want except—*not* annual. That's for budgets.

Yes, planning is hard work. But the alternative is for the church to be wafted to and fro, buffeted by every unforeseen circumstance and blown off course. "We are lost!" wailed a Board member of an unplanned church. "How can we possibly be lost" replied another member, "when we aren't going anywhere?"

Without quantitative goals, clearly understood and widely supported, vigorous progress is unlikely and probably impossible. But they must be the *congregation's* goals because it is the congregation that will make the plan work, not the planners.

Beware the two mistakes of extremes: asking the congregation to do either all the thinking or none. Steer a clear course between Scylla and Charybdis. The best way to make mistake number one is send out a questionnaire to the members asking them what they would like to see the church do.

THE CAMPAIGN BATTING ORDER

Do not dilute the top committee with members of lesser financial stature.

G ET YOUR HEAVY HITTERS up first. I can hardly give you better advice about how to insure the success of a fund-raising campaign. Only those who make (1) the largest, and (2) the most generous gifts should be asked to undertake campaign leadership. Please note (1) largest, *and* (2) most generous. Neither qualification can atone for weakness in the other. Note that the conjunctive is *and*, not or.

Any really ambitious campaign is both a spiritual adventure and a financial exercise. Clap with only one hand and you will probably lose both objectives.

In a manner of speaking, your earliest move is to turn over responsibility for the success of the campaign to those laity whose leadership alone can assure success. Be aware that when the church asks or advises a family to give what will usually be the largest gift it has ever made to anything, the church is preferring both spiritual *and* financial advice; the financial advice is how to invest their money. And, in this, you must enlist the financially most successful of your members right at the top—and early.

Further, only when the big gifts are in will the congregation have confidence that the campaign can succeed. Only when the top financial types assume leadership in building the campaign organization will you have an army adequate to its mission.

You may be tempted, and even often advised, to put generous, financially middle-class members at the top of the batting order. Don't do it. The leaders of the campaign must have two qualifications: (1) financial ability to make a very large gift—one for at least 10 percent of the total campaign goal and (2) commitment to that goal. Now of these two qualifications, which one must the prospective leader bring with him, and which is it your (the church's) responsibility to develop? Or, would you rather select a rich member committed to the cause or make a member of modest financial capability a millionaire?

To lead, in a financial campaign is to step out first rather than waiting for others.

No person involved in the campaign should be expected to solicit a gift larger than his own. Financial influence flows downhill. So if you organize campaign leadership from among your middle-capability members, who will bring in the really big gifts without which you cannot win?

You almost certainly have financially-capable members with little or no record of service. You might be inclined to pass them by in organizing the campaign but that would be a mistake. The largest single reason that financially-capable members have not served is that they have never been asked.

I learned this lesson early when the obviously best-qualified member for the campaign chairmanship not only had never served in any capacity for his church but he was financially so powerful that he intimidated the governing Board. I finally persuaded the Board to go after him any-how. The pastor and three Board members went and asked him to serve. He said nothing for a bit; then he took out a pencil and paper and asked, "Now, who should I have for my committee?"

One reason that many potentially big hitters have not served their church is that they will take only important positions; they are accustomed to delegate, within their own organizations, everything but the most important responsibilities. The paramount rule here is, "Never ask a person to do for the church what he delegates in his own company or profession."

You have to get your heavy hitters at the top of the batting order because somehow (I am amazed that this is so) the members instinctively know that without those very big gifts the campaign cannot win.

Your high-powered campaign committee (by whatever name) must report directly and exclusively to the governing Board.

Do not dilute this top committee with members of lesser financial stature. If you can't avoid it, at least make them ad hoc and without a vote. The minister, of course, is an exception. The minister must be there because many laity agree to serve so that they can get closer to him/her.

FIRST CENTURY COMMUNICATIONS

Only the person who has experienced the gospel of good giving and made a decision to live as a good giver can convey that gospel and secure good pledges.

HATE FUND RAISING THOUGH you might, there's one thing to be said for it. It is the most easily and clearly evaluated thing your church ever does. Dollars are so countable!

Perhaps the strongest contrast between a right and a wrong way, when you count what is produced, is the difference between wholesaling and retailing advice about giving. Wholesaling is what the publicity practitioners call reliance on third-party communication—the insertion of a medium between those who speak and those who listen.

Media provide little or no opportunity for feed-back. All one can say for media is that they are faster and cheaper than person-to-person conversations.

In the first century, Christianity consisted of a few small colonies of believers scattered around the eastern Mediterranean. The members, for the most part, were nobodies. Individual Christians mostly had no influence, less wealth, and even a negative public "image" as we say in our sophistication today.

But within a few centuries—not long, as the history of the world goes—they overcame the mightiest empire that the world had ever seen, and they did it without a printing press. No radio, no TV. They didn't even have a mimeograph, much less a photocopier. No mass media, no weekly bulletins, no impersonalism.

They did it by personal address, by person-to-person talking about what mattered most—their souls. And they overcame the world—or at least their part of it.

The difference between direct address and third-party communication is the difference between two-way and one-way conversations. And perhaps we are now sufficiently advanced to go back to first-century communications—to get back to primitive Christian communications. I do not suggest that you eschew printing presses and dispose of your copier. Third-party communication does have its place. But its place isn't changing lives. It isn't helping the individual member to make a life-changing decision. It isn't for helping anybody decide how much to give.

Our members are inundated with third-party communications. Television and radio commercials, advertisements in newspapers and magazines, on billboards, even (gasp!) sky writing, and our mailboxes are stuffed with letters addressed to "Resident." One-way communications all.

What individual persons need is not impersonal "messages" but person-to-person talk. Generically, what most persons require more of is love. But, even broader than that, what most is required is recognition as individual, distinctive human beings. Of all organizations on this planet, the church is the one that ought to—and in theory does—recognize the infinite value and variety of individual personality. Alas, what we have so much in practice are congregational mailings that might as well be addressed "To whom it may concern."

We professionals cry our eyes out on the vast amounts of time and money that are expended by most churches in self-managed fund-raising campaigns. Treating members *en masse* is wholesaling advice about giving. In a recent survey of persons who had given a million dollars or more to anything, they rated printed literature among the factors that influenced them the least.

The typical every-member canvass is not an every-member anything. It blinks the important fact that each family of the church is at a different stage in the development of its stewardship understanding and performance, and that each family has different financial situations and anxieties. Admonitions to be generous, or to give as the Lord has blessed you, aren't much help to the sincere Christian family struggling with a deficit budget (as most of us are) but asks in all honesty: "How much should we give?" Answers addressed to the congregation at large are seldom helpful to any one family.

There is no substitute—certainly not in Christian churches—for individual conversations in the homes. Great giving decisions, and great gifts, are products of great conversations.

But one caution. Only the person who has experienced the gospel of Jesus and made a decision to live as a Christian can convey the gospel and secure decisions. And only the person who has experienced the gospel of good giving and made a decision to live as a good giver can convey that gospel and secure good pledges. In both cases, that kind of communication is beyond eloquence.

12

A POWER ORGANIZATION

The most creative act that the church performs in the campaign comes before the campaign: creating an organization of great—even if only ad-hoc great—givers.

A T THE RISK OF boring you, I repeat that the power of a campaign organization is based in (1) the size, and (2) generosity of the gifts of its members. You may be saddened by the absence of other criteria. But rise above your sorrow and, if you want to win, build through your tears on only these two bases. The fund-raising power within your church consists of those members who have (1) upper-level giving capability and have (2) personally experienced the Gospel of Good Giving.

Most people are afraid of giving, but your fund raisers

are not. They are, in fact, actual or potential evangelists for the Gospel of Good Giving.

The trouble is that you don't have enough of these qualified and emancipated sort of born-againers to constitute a fund raising campaign organization. So you must create good ad hoc givers—givers to this campaign. That process can bring your qualified fund-raisers up to the necessary quality.

Even so, the temptation to build too large an organization is strong. Stifle it! The chances that you can build and manage a large *and* powerful organization are slim unless you have a professional campaign manager. The traditional ratio of one visitor for each five families is too high. Aim at it, if you must, but settle for much less. There are four reasons why you should be content with less:

1. The campaign organization will be solicited within itself, so subtract that number from families to be visited by the organization.

2. Some 5 percent to 10 percent of the families will be solicited in advance of the campaign by the big gifts committee. So subtract that number.

3. You don't have to visit everybody. Inactive members, non-residents, those living below the poverty line—these can be phoned or written for their pledges.

4. Most visitors will see more than five families if they are encouraged to do so and these will be your best producers. Professional managers will go as high as 1:10. Don't try that on your own, but 1:7½ is all right.

I am often asked how we keep unqualified givers out of the campaign organization. It's easy. You combine the subjects of (1) the gift and (2) serving in the campaign organization into a single subject. But make certain that the prospect knows that only good givers are invited to join the campaign organization.

The most creative act that the church performs in the campaign comes before the campaign: creating an organization of great—even if only ad hoc great—givers.

All the training, all the inspiring messages, all the rah! rah! rah! will not substitute for an organization that (1) has substantially above-average giving capability, and (2) is heavily committed to this campaign as evidenced by its own gifts.

I know one professional campaign manager who sees to it that the campaign organization is built according to the directions that I am trying to give you in this chapter—and then leaves town, confident that, in his words, "This organization cannot lose."

I would not recommend that you try that. Not quite yet.

After the victorious campaign, you can go about converting newly-discovered ad hoc leaders and givers to a more permanent status. In fact, your opportunities to do just that will be glorious.

Happy campaigning!

13

FINANCIAL LEADERS

If you don't get the mega-gifts first, you won't get good gifts from the rest of your congregation.

I OFTEN HEAR, "WE don't want rich, nominal leaders no matter how big their gifts. We want *working* leaders."

What that statement really means is that one wants not leaders, but workers. Who, then, will lead? Who will devise the strategy and call the shots? Who will build the campaign organization? Who will get the big gifts—the Board? The Finance Committee? Who will be ultimately responsible—you?

The way to start is with the members who can make the largest gifts, then see that they do make them. They will then proceed to secure the other biggest gifts and build the campaign organization on the highest possible financial level.

My teacher, the legendary Lewis G. Wells, in making a new-business call on the Board Chair of a large church contemplating a ten-figure building fund, asked "What is your plan for raising this big goal?" To Lew's surprise, the Chair was comfortable with the question. He said, "The Board thinks that we will give one-third, we will get our close friends among the membership to give one-third, and then we will conduct a campaign for the final third." Lew thanked him and left. This fellow knew what he was doing. (All members of the Board were wealthy.)

Every major fund-raising program has two responsibilities: (1) the spiritual development of the members through their making perhaps the largest gifts that they have ever made to anything, and (2) achieving the dollar-amount goal. But if you don't get the megagifts first, you won't get good gifts from the balance of the congregation; thus, your spiritual impact will be weak and you won't reach your goal.

Build your campaign organization from the top down, in descending order according to the size of its members' gifts. The reason for this is that nobody should seek another's gift that should be larger than his own.

People tend to take spiritual advice only from those whom they recognize as qualified to give it. They also tend to take financial advice from those whom they recognize as qualified to give it. They will resist or ignore financial advice from those whom they consider unqualified to give it. You are the official, recognized financial adviser. Members recognize as qualified financial advisers only other members who are their financial superiors or, at the very least, on their own financial level.

Working leaders? You seldom see the president of the local bank at a teller's window, or the Chair of a big manufacturing company working on a turret lathe. These executive types must learn to delegate everything except what only they can do and are responsible for. Any of them who cannot won't long remain chief executives.

Remember that most of your members spend most of their time in the secular world—the world of money. When the church aspires to move their giving from near the bottom of the family budget to at or near the top, you are in fact advising them how to spend or invest an important part of their income or assets. It is a common error to have a financially humble tither call on a member who is financially far above the other's station. No matter how on fire the humble tither about the project or about giving, he cannot importantly influence his financial superiors.

For these reasons you want your heaviest hitters at the top of the batting order.

There are hidden bonuses for you in all this. You will get to know your top financial members better by working with them and they will get to know you better. Each will benefit. Also, your heavy hitters will give more to a campaign for which they are responsible. Many a major church philanthropist was reborn in the process of leading an important campaign on the parish level.

P.S. About my use of the word "gifts." That is okay in talking about raising capital funds. However, when raising operating funds; i.e. the annual every-member canvass, just change "gifts" to "pledges" and carry on.

14

YOUR UNEMPLOYED MILLIONAIRES

Too often we seek for top positions the willing rather than the best qualified.

I F YOU ARE A middle-sized church you probably have at least a few millionaires. Estimates vary, but not much; they average about 1:400. In many churches these wealthy persons are mostly unemployed—so far as church work is concerned. That may be no disaster in some kinds of church work but in fund raising it is catastrophic.

These members should be the top of your campaign batting order: the first to accept positions of top leadership and the first to give.

The classic definition of stewardship embraces "time,

talent, and treasure." Today let's concentrate on talent. It is a noble thing to lay your finest talent on the altar of your God.

Your financial heavy hitters have prime financial influence within the congregation. By assuming leadership and making early, generous gifts they can set the tone for the entire campaign. Their example constitutes an endorsement: "This is an important project. It is a good investment. We can win."

Why do so few of the wealthiest members take the lead in fund raising? Among the many reasons, most of them valid, here are the big three:

1. *The uninvited.* Maybe they haven't been invited.

2. *Small goals.* Maybe they think that the goal is not big enough to require them.

3. *Inadequate staff work.* Maybe they tried it once before but preparation, administration, and staff support were so poor that the campaign failed. Or maybe the big decisions were already, and possibly incorrectly, made.

There are others, but if you check yourself out on these three, the odds are nine out of ten you will know why your heavy hitters don't want even to get on the team.

This is the biggest reason. Too often we seek for top positions the willing rather than the best qualified. Strike one?

Principal executives of large corporations—and even principal owners of small businesses—must learn to delegate. If they won't, they won't be chief executives for long or their small businesses won't be around. An executive must learn to delegate all except only what he (or increasingly she) can do. When you ask a heavy hitter to lead a campaign to raise only a small percentage of what the church really could do—like inching forward 10 percent a year in budget pledges—he delegates in the only way that he can: by refusing to take the job. Strike two?

Campaigns, like any fund raising programs, are won or lost in the planning and preparation. A sharp prospective campaign leader will know, upon sight, if the campaign is properly planned and prepared. Also, heavy hitters should not be required to do their own staff work. They are usually surrounded by competent staff in their own businesses or professions. It is best to employ an outside, professional campaign manager. He or she is not to be a leader but writes the campaign plan, makes all meeting arrangements, oversees the campaign office, and advises and assists the top leaders. Strike three?

There is another consideration: how do you ask your heavy hitters to step out and be at the top of the batting order? This is a vital consideration. Do you want never to hear the deadly "no"?

If your first choice turns you down, you have to go your second choice—well, nobody likes to be second choice and you are in trouble.

15

THE WONDERFUL WORLD OF BIG GIFTS

**What does attract big money? Big, bold,
well-thought out plans for achieving something
important—important to donors.**

Y OUR CHURCH SHOULD occasionally receive a single
gift approximately as large as your entire annual operating budget. Many secular non-profit organizations do.
The largest gifts to secular nonprofit organizations are
made from the capital of the giver to a capital fund of the
organization. Capital to capital—that is, for most
churches, unemployed but important territory.

Raising capital funds—such as building funds—through
the budget is like pedaling a bicycle with one foot. Your po-

tential for capital funds is approximately as large as your potential for budget funds.

Every year, the American Association of Fund Raising Counsel publishes a list of the largest gifts known for the preceding year. Rarely does a church-controlled organization appear on this list; even more rarely does a national religious body; and still more rarely an individual church.

Why not? Because we have become too budget-funds conscious. Yet, the slowest, most expensive , and most agonizing way to create your church's capital funds—such as building funds—is through the budget.

You may not aspire to make the American Association of Fund-Raising Counsel's million-dollar list but you probably could. If you have 426 families, at least one of them is probably a millionaire. True, a family with only $1 million is not a prospect for a gift of $1 million. But it is a prospect for a *bequest* of $1 million. About half of the largest reported gifts, U.S.A., each year are in the form of bequests.

Why do the largest gifts go almost exclusively to secular nonprofit organizations rather than to ecclesiastical bodies? For three reasons, none of which need be an impediment to you in securing ultra-large gifts from your members' capital to the church's capital.

1. The successful secular nonprofit organizations have *big* plans for effectively utilizing big money.

2. They work on fund raising *all year round.*

3. *They ask* for big gifts.

There should be no limit to the amount of money that a church could spend in the Lord's work. But to receive big money, you must have big plans, work on fund raising all year around, and ask for big gifts.

1. BIG PLANS. We often hear the complaint that big gifts go to already successful organizations. The big, downtown church receives a bequest of a million dollars, while

its sister churches that are struggling for survival continue to struggle. But the point is that, from the donor's standpoint, successful organizations have demonstrated their ability to utilize big money effectively; whereas, the little, struggling organizations (religious or secular) have not. "Them as has, gets" is an observation founded in reality. And, as I have been preaching for years—and I sometimes wonder if anybody is listening—*people don't give to needs,* anyway.

Needs do not attract big money. Needs attract alms. What *does* attract big money? Big, bold, well-thought-out plans for achieving something important—important to donors.

2. ALL YEAR ROUND. In the typical church it is open season on giving for about two weeks a year, during the every-member canvass. But the universities, museums, medical centers, *et al* work on fund raising 52 weeks a year. That's a 26-to-1 advantage. It takes any philanthropist a year to decide to give $1 million. You have to stay with it, in season and out. You can't win by talking with him just two weeks out of 52.

3. ASK. Have you ever *asked* for a million-dollar gift? Few really big gifts are made spontaneously. Ask and it shall be given you. Not every time. But often enough. You won't hit a home run every time at bat. But you won't strike out every time, either; not if you have big-enough plans, well thought out, for accomplishing something important, and not if you work all year round on asking.

(I hope, reverend, that when I use "you" herein I mean you the church, not you the pastor. I do not approve of pastors asking for money. What I do mean is your seeing to it that the best-qualified laity are properly charged with responsibility for fund-raising; it is *they* whom I address through you.)

I will pray that you might be spared the ultimate negative lesson in church capital fund-raising. A pastor friend of mine asked a wealthy member to give $1,000 to a special church project, knowing in his heart that he was asking too much. He was refused. In the next morning's newspaper he read that said member had just contributed $1.5 million to his alma mater.

American citizens, corporations, and foundations contributed a record $47.74 *billion* to recognized nonprofit organizations in 1980. The largest 25 bequests of record accounted for $57 million. There were over 200,000 bequests. I wonder, were any of your members among them?

16

THE ONE, BIG-GIFT CAMPAIGN

The prospective donor should have assets of at least ten times the amount of the gift that you seek or surplus income of that amount over the next few years.

THE NEXT TIME YOU want to build a new building, found a new church or mission, or create an endowment for some big community or mission service, give some thought to the possibility of raising the money from a single gift.

No, I have not lost my mind. Big universities, medical centers, and other secular nonprofit organizations do it all the time. In fact, among the successful seculars there is nothing unusual about it.

Many a pastor, when I broached this possibility, replied,

"But I want the whole congregation to feel responsible, and to have the credit and glory." Oh, very well, if you must. But at least finish this article before you flatly reject the big, one-gift campaign.

For one thing, a proper congregation-wide fund raising campaign takes heaps of time, is expensive, and can be very wearing on you.

You may say, "We'll conduct an orthodox campaign and then, if we raise only half or two-thirds or whatever of the goal, go to our richest family and ask them to complete the fund." That is all right except that it is backwards; it is going uphill all the way.

First, you must identify your best prospect. This might take some doing. The Board can take on this chore (or you can seek the advice of the best friend you have in the congregation who is most likely to know. Warning: members who are themselves not wealthy don't know.)

The prospective donor (person or family, usually a family) should have assets of at least ten times the amount of the gift that you seek or surplus income of that amount over the next few years.

Keep this search dark; do not listen to those who say that you have no millionaires in the church. You have. Remember the Texan who almost got control of the silver market, "A billion dollars isn't what it used to be." As I have pointed out, if you have 500 members and are not in a slum you probably have several millionaires.

When the gift has been made and announced, if it was given by the second wealthiest family there is one family in your flock whose feelings are going to be hurt.

Mind you, your search is for ability to give, not generosity, interest in the church, or anything else. Just the giving ability.

Now, gather all relevant information about the prospect.

Family, business, boards of directors, best friends on or near his or her level, financial advisers, important gifts that have been made to anything, interests. You should collect a fairly big file. If you have never done this before, see if you have a fund-raising manager or consultant among the members, or in a higher office within your denomination, who knows how to do it. It is remarkable how much financial and business information is in the public domain—available without snooping—if you know where to look.

Also, of course, assemble the prospective giver's entire record as a member of the church—attendance, service, giving, interests.

Now, assemble and organize all information about the project. This file should include what will happen if the church does this thing—builds this building, establishes the fund, or whatever. What will happen if we do it. What will happen if we don't. Why we are not going to conduct an every-member fund-raising campaign. (Expensive, time-consuming, and maybe we would fail.)

Who within the congregation is best-qualified to present the invitation to make this wonderful gift? Don't rush this one. It is as important as it was to select the prospective donor. It should be the person whom the prospect most respects—especially on financial matters.

You may want some back-up persons on this such as the prospect's banker, accountant, member of the family, solicitor. Do not include yourself. Look for "common boards," that is, those who sit on various corporate or other boards of directors whose approval of the prospect's making this gift might add weight to the making of the presentation.

Finally, decide how the gift is to be recognized. The most common way is to name the building or the fund. But you will think of other ways, also. Do not assume that the donor will want no recognition. Do not even agree with the donor when recognition is rejected. On the other hand, it is just possible that the donor may want to make the gift a memorial, and you can agree to that.

There is no standard procedure here. I can only advise that this isn't going to be a one-visit matter. A wealthy person gives just as much time and thought to giving a million dollars as to investing it. Have patience. I cannot even tell you if only one person should do the asking or two—but never more than two at the first presentation and not even that many at-a-time thereafter. That is all that I can tell you on this subject. Most important—don't rush the process.

A few more don'ts. Don't have a second choice ready in case the prospect says no. The presenter must respond to the prospect's almost inevitable question, "Who else do you have in mind for this?" with "Nobody" and look the prospect right in the eye.

You stay off the firing line. If you have been reading these articles of mine recently you will know that you, the pastor, must never ask a member for money for the church. You will be tempted, but you must resist.

Keep quiet about even the fact that the presentation has been made until the action is all over and the gift has been promised—whether by this or any other prospect.

Throughout this chapter I have said "You" do this or that. I do not expect that you will conduct the planning, research, and strategizing all by yourself.

I hope that you can get professional help on this matter. You are probably not a graduate student in the art and science of fund raising. Even so, remember my previous admonitions that if you ask, it is begging, because it is the church asking, whereas when a layperson asks, the especially if properly, that is fund raising.

17

HAPPY MONEY

We must beware of taking the voluntary element out of giving.

SOME MONEY IS SAD money, some is is happy money. Sad money is paid as a duty, or for benefits long since obtained, or as a penalty. Taxes, debt-payments, fines—these are paid with sad money.

Unfortunately, many church members respond to stewardship appeals with sad money. They see church giving as a duty, and duty is a grim subject. "Oh Duty! Why has thou not the visage of a sweetie or a cutie?" *(Ogden Nash)* We aggravate the misunderstanding, regardless of our good intentions, when we tell the members that their money isn't theirs, that it belongs to God, and that they have a duty to give some of it back to the church. That takes all the fun out of giving!

"Specifically, the doctrine that stewardship is an obligation imposed by divine decree can have little motivating force." (Dr. LeRoy T. Howe)

We must beware of taking the voluntary element out of giving. The church did that in the Middle Ages and bred an inevitable revolution. If we aren't going to encourage 100 percent voluntary giving, we might as well follow the example of our Jewish friends: charge dues, have done with it, and avoid pious language.

You spend happy money when you spend more than you know you should on your loved one's birthday present. Happy-money giving is generous giving. Peter Marshall once said that he had decided to increase his church giving to show the Lord how much he loved him. But then he hastily corrected himself: "No, it is to show *me* how much I love *him.*" I can still see how happy he looked.

Happy-money giving means joy to both the receiver and the giver. The greater, the more generous the gift, the greater the joy. But sad-money giving produces only pain, or perhaps a yawn.

We also err when we motivate giving by pleading the church's needs. Giving to needs isn't fun and it doesn't generate happy money. What's more, it isn't even effective. "If you're going to talk needs, the family always has more needs than the church." *(Ferdinand Fletcher)*

"Money flows best toward high standards, bold goals, and completely dedicated leadership." *(Sy Seymour)* High standards, bold goals, and dedicated leadership generate happy money. This is illustrated by the remarkable amounts of money that a church can raise—that its members will give—in a popular and well-managed building-fund campaign. A study of 5,500 church building-fund campaigns shows that, using separate three-year pledges, the members of 85 percent of American and Canadian churches will give as much to the building fund as to the budget within that three year period; and the members of about 15 percent of the churches will give *twice* as much. Yet the members of most of those churches had been increasing their budget giving by only about 10 percent a year.

The members of a congregation that are giving happy money will get along much better with each other, and love their church more, than a congregation that is giving sad money. There is an exhilaration in being part of an achieving congregation, and the contagion of happy giving within the church family is lovely to behold.

For we are not Simeon Stylitus, a Christian alone on a pedestal in the desert; we are members of a congregation—a church family—and each of us influences the other more than he knows. One can be a great giver, and be lonesome in his giving, and that doesn't produce as much happiness as being part of a family of happy givers. Your happiest givers make your best fund raisers.

As pastor, you can encourage happy giving both on an individual basis and on a congregational basis. Each effort will augment the other.

We also err when we shroud all church giving in secrecy and painstakingly protect the members from all knowledge about what anybody else is giving. True, there is giving for recognition, and that is unwholesome. But it is rare. Absolute secrecy assumes that most of the giving around here is nominal—that it is sad money, even ashamed money—and that assumption in a church is usually right.

But there is joy in wholesome recognition, especially if it is not sought. "The greatest pleasure I know is to do a good

action by stealth and have it found out by accident."
(Charles Lamb) The secular nonprofit organizations seem to
know this better than we do. They certainly receive larger
gifts. As a stewardship leader, you mature the day that you
open your newspaper and learn that one of your members
who has been giving you $5 a week has given his alma ma-
ter a million-dollar building—with his name on it.

We are less secretive about giving in a building-fund
campaign than in every-member canvasses. Perhaps that is
one reason why we can raise so much more in building-
fund campaigns. Most building-fund money is happy
money. One pastor, observing this, mourned, "If only we
could raise as much for what goes on in a building as for
the building!" But we can.

You might want to resolve that you will seek only happy
money for your church.

Set your happy-money goal high and order your victory
banners now! Celebrate! Because giving happy money is a
celebration in both the sacred and profane meanings of the
word.

18

YOUR CHURCH IS NOT A CHARITY

A good gift is one that has a positive effect on the spiritual development and life of the giver.

Y OU CAN TAKE CREDIT on your income tax return for what you give your church as a "charitable contribution" but your church is not a charity. Let us not confuse IRS jargon with holy writ. Let us not confuse almsgiving with giving to the church.

CHARITY: Acts of charity done to the poor . . . or helpless. *(Oxford)* Benevolent actions of any sort for the needy. *(Random House)*

ALMS: Charitable relief of the poor. *(Oxford)* Money, food, or other donations given to the poor or needy. *(Ran-*

dom House) Something—as money or food—given to the poor or needy. *(Merriam Webster)*

It is time that we got ourselves straightened out on the difference between a charity and the church, and between almsgiving and giving. The church is not—or at least should not—be poor, helpless, needy, or suffering. The church doesn't—or at least should not—ever seek alms. The church is not a beggar. The mendicant posture ill becomes it. So let us stand erect.

True, our great-grandfathers, many of our grandfathers, even some of our fathers were paid in sacks of potatoes and hand-me-down clothing. The typical country parson was expected to be grateful for whatever he got. He *was* poor, helpless, needy, and if he was not suffering his wife surely was.

But that era is past, and good riddance. So long as the pastor is supported by alms, he cannot perform his essential role as spiritual adviser. One might give, but one does not take, advice on anything from a beggar. Few church members are so advanced spiritually as to take advice from the poor, sometimes not even from the penniless Nazarene.

The subject of giving to the church has been so larded over with pious language that the church has unknowingly worked itself into the position of being grateful for *any* contribution, into seemingly accepting that any contribution is a good thing. But almsgiving to one's church is not a good thing.

For years I deprecated almsgiving to the church as tipping the church, but I have had to give that up lately. A common tip for a good, middle-class meal is now more than the average church member's weekly contribution to his church. The church, all unknowingly, is still in the position of saying that any contribution is a good contribution.

But what is a good contribution? Surely not alms. Surely not just any gift. My definition: a good gift is one that has a positive effect on the spiritual development and life of the giver. And I suppose few will contend that a weekly contribution of $5 is a good gift for a family with $50,000 annual income—assuming income from all sources, including a working wife, which is now the American norm. The elemental consideration is not how much the contribution helps the church, but *how much it helps the giver.*

The trouble is that we have not yet really gotten through to most members that the Gospel of Good Giving is real. We are still talking too much about the needs of the church, and about giving as a duty, and not enough about the spiritual necessity of the member to give. We have unthinkingly and wrongly slid into accepting the role of the church as a charity. As we advance toward our proper role as spiritual advisers and advocates of the Gospel of Good Giving—the good news for the giver that it really is better to give than to receive, better for the giver—we are dragging along with the IRS concept of all giving as charity, and of almsgiving as giving.

We have not yet communicated our Gospel of giving as well as the IRS has communicated its definition of good giving.

What to do about it?

Well, for starters let's give up begging—stressing the need of the church to receive—in favor of proclaiming that it really *is* better to give than to receive. After all, we do have a clear biblical basis for asserting that.

And let us not forget that where our members' treasure is, there will their hearts be also: in church.

19

THE COURAGE TO FAIL

The mortal enemy of success in capital fund raising is not over-goaling but fear of failure. And yet, what is there to fear about failure?

W HEN IT COMES TO estimating how much their church can raise, most Boards are composed of two kinds of experts: optimists and pessimists. If your Board is like most, the pessimists outnumber the optimists. If the fund required is very much larger than what the church has ever raised before, both estimates are usually too low.

The optimists tend to be good givers; the pessimists tend to be token givers. The optimists, especially the self-made types, are likely to be entrepreneurs and probably success-ful; the pessimists lean more to fixed incomes. The optimists mostly have experience in handling large amounts of money; the pessimists mostly have not.

Surprisingly, both groups include those experienced and inexperienced in church leadership, although the inexperienced optimists have an edge here; the pessimists are inclined to say that we tried raising money in 1942 and it didn't work or, even more deadly, "This isn't a good time to raise money."

Frequency of church attendance seems to be a neutral factor.

I once attended a meeting of a church Board at which a large and long-debated capital expenditure was voted down; this, despite the advocacy of the wealthiest member present. The pastor and I sat there pained and helplessly quiet because we knew in confidence that said Board member had already decided to give the whole amount if the Board voted to go ahead. "Nothing ventured, nothing gained" to quote an old apothegm.

A strange but provable truth is that when Board members vote whether to essay a big building fund, they are not estimating what the congregation will give; they are estimating what they, themselves will give—in money and in fund raising effort.

There is a sort of quirky wisdom about this process because the resolve with which the Board sets the church on a program has everything to do with how much will be raised.

Thus, the Board almost always seriously under-estimates how much it can raise if it engages the program on a high level of commitment and then does everything by the book. Why this is so is no mystery; the Board has had more experience—possibly its total experience—with campaigns entered upon in the spirit of, "Well, let's give it a go. Who knows, it might succeed."

The production of an all-out program to raise the church's maximum potential can be more accurately predicted—and is more likely to succeed—than a more modest enterprise.

For instance, for years I have estimated at least once a week the capital fund-raising potential of a church that needs as much capital funds as it can raise. I do this quite accurately when I have the essential data. (About 75 percent of American and Canadian churches can raise from three to six times their undesignated contributions to the annual operating budgets. The science, of course, comes down to finding where, between $3 \times$ and $6 \times$, a particular church can produce.) But what a church will raise for a goal that the Board considers a piece of cake I cannot predict nor can anybody else. For one thing, a campaign thus entered upon is quite likely to end up in disaster city, and who wants to predict a disaster?

The myth endures that it is easier to raise a small than a large goal. But if a smaller goal is thought to be easy, your strongest prospective fund-raising leaders will not take campaign leadership positions (what's the challenge or glory in leading a project that purportedly can't lose?) and the members will not give as much thought to, "How much shall I give?" (HMSIG) They also won't pray about it and, within my experience, that makes all the difference in the world.

The mortal enemy of success in capital fund raising is not over-goaling but fear of failure. And yet, what is there to fear about failure?

Even in the high jump, you get three tries. (If at first you don't succeed. . .) And if you never knock the bar off, how will you know how high you can jump? If you lose not one game all season, aren't you playing in the wrong league? If you gain ground every down, perhaps you are selecting your opponents on the wrong basis. If you always break the tape first, OK; but are you setting any records?

To succeed magnificently, have the courage to fail. You are not just a leader, you are a Christian leader.

20

TEACHING CHURCHES NOT TO BEG

**We placed increasing emphasis on the need of the
giver to give rather than on the need of
the church to receive.**

U NTIL SHORTLY AFTER THE end of World War Two, there was no distinctive technique of church fund raising. The churches conducted annual every-member canvasses for contributions to annual operating budgets just as they had done since the early 1920s. ("Like a mighty tortoise/Moves the church of God/Brothers we are treading/ where we've always trod.")

Meanwhile, the secular nonprofit organizations made big strides. They shifted emphasis from number of gifts to size, introduced the concept of long-range financial development, opened the field of planned (originally "deferred") gifts, created and popularized the vocations of fund-raising consultants and campaign managers.

Two simultaneous events shook the churches out of their apathy: (1) a gigantic surge in interest in religion and participation in churches, and (2) a shortage of essential building materials before, during, and even for a short time after the war prevented the churches from new construction. When these materials did again become available, the pent-up need for more buildings could be met if the churches could pay for them.

Aye, there's the rub.

Just then under the leadership of our resident genius, a few of us founded Wells Organizations. We all knew community fund raising cold. Lew Wells had managed some 60 Community Chest (as they were known in those days) campaigns and won every one of them. He was often our teacher and always our leader. We specialized exclusively in church clientele.

Within a very few years we had 44 offices in North America, and five overseas; 190 full-time North American campaign managers and another 60 overseas. We managed 5,300 building fund campaigns and 500 budget funds with a win record varying from 93 percent to 97 percent. Our seven-pound campaign manager's manual, chairmen's notebooks, the pledge card, and many other materials for individual-church adaptation became standard for the industry.

As we progressed, we placed increasing emphasis on the need of the giver to give rather then on the need of the church to receive; on the idolatry of worshiping one's dollars; on giving as an investment (Where your treasure is . . .). We advertised not only in religious publications, but also in *Fortune* magazine what we came to call "The Gospel of

Good Giving." We quoted only Jesus. Our rabbi friends forgave us.

But all this was superimposed on a detailed, tested, and ultimately complete technology. Neither sublimated motives for giving nor the technologies of administration and organization can substitute for the other.

We taught our client churches not to beg: not for time, not for talents, not for treasure. As for token or nominal giving, we contrasted that with good giving in our often re-published, "A Farewell to Alms."

Wells was built on the rising tide of the churches for capital—especially building—funds. We never made the transition to operating funds for one reason: the churches mostly knew that they could not self-manage capital campaigns that were geared to raise from three to seven times, in three-year pledges, what the congregations were currently pledging to their annual operating budgets. But they thought that budget giving levels and habits were cast in concrete. We proved this to be wrong, but never popularized the point. We had no sense of history, so we affected almost entirely our client churches and let the rest of the world go by.

So far as national and international influence goes, our manuals, materials, and methods are today about as influential as the Rosetta Stone. But it is high time for these tablets to be re-displayed.

21

SPEAK TO MY CONCERNS

Great gifts are the product of great conversations, and they had better be on the right subject: what concerns the giver.

J AMES GREGORY LORD, FUND-RAISING consultant to secular institutions, tells that at the end of a campaign he asked the General Chair, "What could I have done to be more helpful?" The Chair thoughtfully responded, "Give each volunteer more information about each prospect." Good advice.

In church fund-raising we are well-started in the right direction because we encourage members of the campaign organization to select those on whom they will call. But we seldom go far enough.

In a major building fund or relocation campaign your lead prospect perhaps could give a million dollars. Consider for a moment to what lengths you will go to understand something of their financial capability, their feelings about the project, the church, and possibly their own spiritual lives; who they best know and respect on their own financial level; what big gifts they have made to anything. You will, of course, have their giving records both to annual operations and any capital campaigns that you have conducted recently. You will know their participation in organizations and activities of the church and what leadership positions they may have held. You should also know on what boards they sit—nonprofit or profit, and especially what banks. Also what element or feature of the new construction they might want to establish as a memorial.

It is financially practical for you to spend all the time necessary to learn this much about a prospect for a million dollars. It is spiritually practical for you to learn this much about any family of the church, regardless of their giving capability. You might ask the lead family to give 5 percent of its net assets when you suggest a million dollars; the decision of a family with net assets of $100,000 to consider giving $5,000, which will be an equivalent gift is just as difficult for them as for the lead family to give a million.

The Right Direction. I do not suggest that you all at once go this deeply into gathering information about every family that will be asked to contribute. But I do suggest that you start moving in this direction. And it may be a good idea to start compiling and organizing what information you can.

What motivated a great gift is a subject usually surrounded by mystery and wrapped in guesswork. Strangely, it does not always help to ask the giver. For one thing, the giver may not know; for another, even knowing, the person might not say. Giving—not just the routine sort of nominal or token giving, not just alms-giving but the kind of giving that changes lives—which is of course what you are after— is a profoundly personal act.

Dangerous Generalization. Yet you must learn what you can. Generalizations about why people give are dangerous. It isn't why you want or expect a person to give but why they in fact do. You can expect that personal spiritual self-fulfillment always plays a part but, even here, tread cautiously. I have spent most of my life preaching the Gospel of Good Giving—that it really is better to give than to receive—but I must admit that, like all generalities about why give, it is not equally applicable in all cases. The person expects or at least hopes that the church will "speak to my concern" but that does not necessarily provide the key to what is the primary concern.

Assuming duty as a motive is a dead end. Most churches will feel that giving is a member's duty. There may be some justification for this but, in the large, it is a mistake, even though it oftens plays a part.

The fundamental point is that most great gifts arise from the church's speaking to the giver's deepest concern. Those wonderful "Friends" with their "Speak to my concern" and each person's "inner light" have it right. Great gifts are the product of great conversations, and they had better be on the right subject: what concerns the giver.

Of course, in a building fund campaign you must have the case statement well in hand: what will happen if we do or don't build; evidence that the church has done all of its homework on site, building plan, costs, et al. But that the cause is right and well thought out is not enough. A wealthy family has a thousand opportunities a year to contribute to good and right causes.

Giving to one's church is not charity. We give that we

may live, and that more abundantly. But where does the member sit within that generality? Remember the old newspaper editor's admonition: "It ain't no use talking to nobody about nuthin' that ain't already on his mind."

22

HOW TO TELL A GOOD GIFT

Refusal to give permission to talk about one's gift
will usually indicate dissatisfaction with the gift.
But never ask for that permission unless
you are reasonably sure that it is a good gift.

ALL QUALIFIED FUND-RAISING consultants and campaign managers insist that a church pre-campaign classify its households according to individual estimated giving ability. The inexperienced sneer at this process but I do not know an expert with 100 campaigns behind him who would enter upon a campaign without it. To conduct a major fund-raising program without evaluations would be like driving a racing car blindfolded: you would not know where you are and whether you are winning or losing.

Yet, as the pledges begin to come in, simply to know

what percentage of evaluation was produced isn't enough. You also want to know if the important giver thought that the gift was good.

Go back. That is what counts because a good gift is best defined by the giver. Also,many a great gift was the result of an increased pledge—occasionally, even for the second time. It may be difficult to believe, but increased pledges frequently win campaigns.

Sy Seymour, the guru of secular fund raising, advised Harvard, when its historic campaign came up about 10 percent short after five years of hard work, "Go back to your biggest givers again." They thought the old fellow was off his rocker but, for lack of agreement on any other course of action, they did as he advised. Within a few months they were over the top. I think that among those increased pledges was David Rockefeller's increase number two.

The great Lewis G. Wells, who practically invented modern church fund raising, said: "A person doesn't break his arm when he signs a pledge card. He can still write." The fact is that most pledgers, as the pen hovers over the card, have two figures in mind: "I know I'll give at least. . ." and "Of course I could go crazy and give as much as. . ." Part of the science or art of fund raising is to get something close to the larger figure on the pledge card. That becomes the pledge of record but the memory of the larger, noble figure lingers on.

It's like decisions that all of us have made over the years; if we had had more evidence, vision, or courage we would have made the more difficult but right decision.

Those who have not had experience with capable consultants or campaign managers think that we have a bag of tricks. We do not; we work from known principles and utilize proven methods. But we do one thing that might be considered a trick.

When we are trying to find if a pledger is through giving, we tell him of a few great pledges already received. If his response is, "Yea, that's nice" and changes the subject, we know that he is not satisfied with his pledge—not yet. But if he (or she, I never referred to Jeanette Rockefeller as "he") says, "Great! That's the kind of giving we need around here," waste no more time on that pledger. He thinks his gift is good, and the odds are that he is right. After all, even with our evaluation process, he knows more about his financial capability than we do.

Of course, you or anybody else must have the pledgers' permission to talk about their gifts. But every good pledger should be asked for that. It is impossible for a congregation to seek a big congregational objective if everybody goes into a closet to sign their pledges, puts them into envelopes and (ugh!) seals them. That congregation may be an audience but it is no congregation.

Refusal to give permission to talk about one's gift will usually indicate dissatisfaction with the gift. But never ask for that permission unless you are reasonably sure that it is a good gift.

Why will a member increase his pledge? Within my experience, it usually comes from learning that his financial peers are giving better than he is. There are other reasons, but I think that this one is prime.

In a recent campaign, one of the financially upper-level members was terribly critical of the campaign right from the start. He grumbled and groused no end. One day he walked into the campaign office, bitched some more, and demanded his signature pledge card back. The campaign manager, a seasoned pro, thought seriously of telling him that he did not know where it was, or any other possible excuse, but then reluctantly handed it over.

As the complainer crossed out $50,000, the campaign

manager's heart lost a beat. When the complainer wrote in $100,000, that doggone heart did a double beat. In a subdued voice, the manager managed one syllable: "Why?" The answer came quickly.

"Because I've been studying the gifts table and I know your four biggest gifts to date and I know that I should be among the five biggest givers to this campaign."

Well, you never know, do you? Not all the good guys wear white hats.

23

YOUR TRUE
FUND-RAISING
POTENTIAL

**Here is a table that measures what your church
should be able to raise.**

H OW MUCH COULD YOUR church raise for a new building, or for some other big objective? What is the
true, all-out giving potential of your congregation? The table on P. 76 will tell you.

The table is derived from computerized analyses of several thousand professionally-managed (but not professional
solicitors, ugh!) building-fund campaigns for three-year
pledges. It is based on the two largest factors affecting how
much a church can raise: (1) the number of identified, undesignated budget-giving families, and (2) how much they

are giving now. There are other factors, to be sure. But these two are so much more important than any of the others that the two-factor base is quite accurate at establishing your conservative minimum

About 92 percent of American and Canadian churches will produce within 15 percent of the table either way, up or down—mostly up. Some churches have doubled it, but not many.

In the left-hand column, find the line that comes closest to the number of your identified giving families. This means, generally, those that have signed pledges or use weekly offering envelopes.

Across the top of the table, find the figure closest to the amount that these families are now giving. Do not include giving to capital fund, special offerings, or designated collections.

For instance, if you have 300 identified giving families you are on line IV. If they are giving $90,000 a year, you are on column D. Live IV and column D cross the box that reads 5.00. This is your factor. Multiply your identified, undesignated budget giving, $90,000, by 5. This produces an amount of $450,000, which is your book potential.

Why do we use building-fund contributions as our guide to potential? Because most churches can raise nearer their maximum capability in a building-fund campaign. Why do we use three-year pledges? Because they produce the maximum amount of actual collections. If you use a shorter pledge-payment period, the members will pledge and give less; if you use more than three-year pledges, your collections will fall off. Why do we specify professional campaign management? Because these campaigns produce the most money.

What about the campaigns that failed? Almost none of them achieved less than 85 percent of the goal. What about the campaigns that exceeded the table? Many of them went 'way over the top.'

What could keep your church from producing on the table? First, of course, would be publishing a lower goal than your indicated capability (in that case, reduce the pledge-payment period). Second, managing the campaign yourselves instead of using experienced management (on-job training here can be costly). Third, a serious schism in the church, because if factions are too busy fighting each other they may not have enough time to win the campaign.

But, given a big-enough published (and valid) goal, not trying a do-it-yourself campaign, and assuming a reasonably healthy church: order your Victory Banners now!

NORMAL MINIMUM BUILDING-FUND POTENTIAL CDC campaign management°three-year pledges							
FAMILES GIVING	**A.** $20,000	**B.** $30,000	**C.** $50,000	**D.** $90,000	**E.** $130,000	**F.** $210,000	**G.** $340,000
VI 890				7.00	5.75	4.50	3.25
V 550			6.75	6.00	4.75	3.50	2.25
IV 340		6.50	5.75	5.00	3.75	2.50	1.25
III 210	6.25	5.50	4.75	4.00	2.75	1.50	
II 130	5.25	4.50	3.75	3.00	1.75		
I 80	4.25	3.50	2.75	2.00			

LATCH ON TO THE AFFIRMATIVE

Almost all budgets are compromised, watered-down and squeezed-out documents. They are negative. They have no power to stir people's souls.

L ET US NOW LOOK at the power of the affirmative where it is most needed and where it produces the most strik-ing results: in budget pledging.

Let's face it: most annual every-member canvasses are a drag. Much talk abounds about the church's needs (al-though the church has no needs); financial crises (which are caused mainly by the Board's bloopers); the pervasive concept of giving as a duty (which produces only alms); or begging (which is demeaning).

Almost all budgets are compromised, watered-down and

squeezed-out documents. They are negative. They have no power to stir people's souls. They are divisive and invite argument. The hard-nosed, confirmed token giver when invited to pledge will cross his arms, rare back, and ask: "What's the budget?" Answer that question and, no matter what you say, you are lost. Tactically, the average budget provides no reason for generous giving and countless excuses for token giving. It is at best hesitant and fearful and at worst static and apologetic.

The annual operating budget is a spending document; it is not a fund-raising document. The budget committee cannot legislate how much the members will give. So eliminate the biggest negative right at the start: eliminate the pre-canvass budget. That will leave the protective token giver without a base on stand on. But it also does much more than that.

Let's replace the dreary, lock-step annual budget with a thoughtfully-prepared list of—not just what the church *must* do to survive but—what it *should* do and even what it *could* do if it got its act together and caught fire. This document is not easily or quickly assembled. It takes time, thought, and patience. Well, sorry about that. But what is leadership? The issue is not whether the church will survive, but whether it will flourish. Okay? Well then, that is the big positive number one: to flourish.

It doesn't matter for how long you plan on the *must, should,* and *could* basis so long as it is not for one year. If you do that, you get right back to the annual operating drag budget. It is my experience that three years is a reasonable minimum, and that much more than five years is difficult to handle.

It is the church victorious, setting bold goals and then striving valiantly to achieve, that can stir people's souls. "See what a great church we are becoming" will beat the stuffings out of "Please give to avert a deficit budget" every time.

In only three centuries or so a bunch of little churches scattered around the eastern Mediterranean conquered the greatest empire ever seen on this planet. And they didn't do it with survival budgets.

Static plans are inherently negative, and a negative cannot produce a positive. If you want positive giving you must have positive, dynamic plans.

As to fund raising, use your financially most influential members for the planning. No standing committees, please. This will take an ad hoc. You had better stay in there, close to this group, making certain that they keep their eyes on the ultimate, that they accent the positive, eliminate the negative, and that they don't mess with Mr. In-between. If you have to work too hard at this, you have selected the wrong committee members. Stay with financially successful members who are not frightened of big numbers—especially big numbers of dollars. Avoid faithful members worn out in service to the church who know what can't be done.

Now, given a bold plan, medium- or long-range, take it to the members. Only after having done a good job of planning and congregational communication are you ready to get into fund raising.

"You've got to AC-cent-tchu-ate the POS-itive, e-LIM-in-ate the NEG-a-tive, hang on to the a-FIRM-a-tive, don't mess with Mr. Inbetween."*

*AC-CENT-TCHU-ATE THE POSITIVE by Harold Arlen and Johnny Mercer copyright 1944 Harwin Music Co. Copyright renewed 1972 Harwin Music Company. International copyright secured. All rights reserved. Used by permission.

25

IS GIVING A SPIRITUAL OR FINANCIAL MATTER?

B OTH. TO COIN AN old phrase, they are two sides of the same coin. To feature only one is like clapping with one hand.

For your members to hear about only the spiritual side is not enough. They may give out of gratitude to God but they must give dollars. Remember that they live in a dominantly financial and fallen world. "How much should we give?" is not a frivolous question.

For your members to hear about only the financial side is to put the church on the same level as all the other million non-profit organizations and institutions that depend upon contributions—and that is not where the church belongs. I propose here to make the case for both sides of the coin as essential.

It isn't so much a question of what the church needs to receive as what the members need to give. The important part of the transaction is its effect on the giver, not its effect on the church. Jesus said that it is better to give than to receive. (Better for the giver, and truer words were never spoken or written.) A life that is all get and no give is self-destructive and sub-human. "We give that we may live, for to withhold is to perish." *(Kahlil Gibran)*

The opposite of generosity is greed. Mammon enters as a slave then moves to guest and finally to master. And he makes a good slave but a bad master. Of all the institutions that ask, there is only one (fragmented though it may be) that bears any responsibility about teaching about giving—the church. If we don't do it, it won't get done and Mammon thrives.

Let's hear Gibran again on this. "There are those who give with joy, and that joy is their reward. And there are those who give and know not pain in giving, nor do they seek joy, not give with mindfulness of virtue. They give as in yonder valley the myrtle breathes its fragrance into space. Through the hands of such as these God speaks, and from behind their eyes he smiles upon the earth."

But the members are not going to give to statements from Gibran, much less from scripture. They are going to give cold cash, bucks, iron men, dollars. And neither Gibran nor scripture are any help on *how many* dollars, or *how* to give. For that reason, you cannot stop with scripture. Your people need help on how and how much. Fund-raising consultants have a key word for this: "HMSIG"— how much should I give?

"Tithe" is not, of itself enough. Not for most Christians.

Nor will *any* single formula suffice. The members need specific, individual help. We can do this for them in various ways.

Especially in capital fund raising, such as for building funds, we can develop a specific, dollar-amount suggestion for each individual family. Not to do this after all the organization and promotion and congregational letters and printed materials, is to turn away from the family at the point of critical mass, look the other way, and say, "You work that out."

We can organize to deliver individual home visits by members who have already made their giving decisions (whether to capital or operating funds) in an exemplary manner. Only good givers can make other good givers.

Advocacy. The best givers should be prevailed upon to tell the congregation—or at least parts of it—(1) what they are giving, (2) why, (3) what they went through in coming to that difficult decision*, and (4) how they feel about it now. Probably more good givers are made this way than in all other ways put together.

Even though it might be painful, stop talking so much about the church's needs. The congregation is not responsible for the needs, the governing Board is. Pleading needs does not belong in the pulpit. People do not become good givers because the church's needs are big, important, or even dramatic. Schuller characterizes this as "Invest in this sinking ship!"

It might help for you to put in headline type and hang on your study wall or cork board: "The member's need to give is more important than the church's need to receive."

That's what I did. It helps.

**This is one reason that the pastor must never solicit gifts or pledges alone, although he or she may accompany a layperson on a few key visits.*

BACK CREDITS

The advantages of the back credits fund raising concept are that it is polite, well-mannered and positive. It honors previous gifts and gives them first place. It says, 'Thank you for what you have already done.'

WHAT SHOULD YOU DO after you conduct a building-fund campaign and fail? You still need the building—not just part of it, all of it. Most churches at this point make the mistake of borrowing the rest of the money needed or cutting back on the building size or quality. Either way, on the surface, may seem to be a reasonable decision, but it is a long way down disaster alley.

If there is one thing that you don't need just now it is a mortgage. For another, if you quit now you will have to live with a conspicuous failure for a long, long while. You will have a discouraged church.

There is a better way.

I did not invent the better way; Lew Wells did that, as he did almost everything else about the fund raising. I was, however, the first to use it, and my students and I have trained a generation of fund-raising managers to use it. The success record is excellent—even better, maybe, than that of original campaigns.

The mistake that you must not make is to think that the campaign has tested the fund-raising ability of the congregation. All fund raising fails, mostly raising only about 25 percent of the church's potential. Your campaign left three times the potential that it raised.

I had just completed a successful campaign for the Little Rock Episcopal downtown church. Down the street, the big First Methodist church was still smarting from a failure to raise the cost of a needed education building. They were impressed, and perhaps encouraged, by the Episcopal results and invited me to manage anther campaign for them. I did.

That second campaign brought their total building fund just up and over the $300,000 objective. (That was in the early 1950s; today it would have been well over a million.)

We added three lines to the new pledge card.

Previously paid $_____

New pledge $_____

TOTAL GIFT $_____

Thus the concept of back credits was born. Ever since, sophisticated church fund-raising managers have known how to handle the results of a failed campaign. To my knowledge, it always succeeds. A standing joke among us professionals is that this would be a great vocation if we could just let the church lose the first campaign and then bring us in to win the second.

The advantages of this system are readily apparent. It is polite, well-mannered, and positive. Instead of brushing aside previous gifts, it honors them; gives them first place. The first thing that a canvasser or solicitor says to the individual family is, "Thank you for what you have already given."

Note that the first-line verb is "paid." When the giver signs a new pledge, any unpaid balance on the original pledge is cancelled.

I like to run the scoreboard on *new* money only for the teams, but total gifts for the public totals board. In conversations and announcements both of totals and of individual contributions, it is best to use the new total figures.

You can conduct the second campaign any time but the strongest time is before the original pledges expire. Unless you are going to wait for a long while between campaigns, don't leave a short gap—overlap a little.

There is no limit that I know of between the time the original and the back-credits campaigns unless you go ahead between times and build with borrowed funds— which is not a bright idea. It won't *kill* the back-credits campaign but it will complicate things and make it more difficult. If you spend some time with this concept of the back-credits campaign you will begin to see the advantages that is has over the original campaign. I'll mention only one: confidence.

All fund raising exists in confidence. And if you raised as little as 51 percent of your goal in the original campaign just about everybody will agree that you can complete the fund in the second campaign. That is a big start.

If you are going to conduct a back-credits campaign write me with any questions about the how: 2230 Lake Park Drive #193, San Jacinto, CA 92383.

ARE WE READY FOR FUND RAISING?

There is no best time to raise funds. They are all bad.

W HEN I WAS OPERATIONS Manager of the largest church fund raising management company, I sought the best time to raise funds. An exhaustive study, with the help of outside consultants, came in with a clear answer.

There is no best time to raise funds. They are all bad.

The trouble is that I was studying the calendar, which has almost nothing to do with the subject. The question is: When are you ready? Answer: When you are prepared. This is almost (not quite) fund-raising lesson number one.

The completely prepared, and *only* the completely prepared, campaign can win. In fact, thoroughly prepared campaigns almost never lose.

I say "almost" because a pre-campaign feasibility study by a competent firm is also a requirement.

The list of eight criteria, herewith, is the product of 40 years' experience. I think that there are no others. I know that all eight are essential.

A. Spending plan. What you have determined upon: a new building, or missions or benevolence fund, or an enlarged total program of organizations and activities.

B. Fund-raising plan. You can save yourself much labor, trouble, and even agony by having a professional firm write this for you. Never use a general pattern plan. Every church is different. Yours is different.

C. Resolution. A document signed by all members of the Governing Board and of the fund raising leadership committee, saying, "I will accept any position in the fund raising organization that the Chair and Pastor ask me to take."

D. Case statement. A brief (never more than 12 pages double-spaced), of what we are going to do, why we are going to do it, what will happen if we do, what will happen if we don't.

E. Prospect list. All members listed, carded, and with essential information therein.

F. Leaders. Top members of the campaign organization.

G. Organization. A chart, table, and list of prospective members of the total fund raising organization.

H. Budget. All costs of the fund raising program.

I said that all times are bad. What I mean is that every time has some disadvantage. There is no time that is absolutely right, so do not waste time searching for it.

The time to go is when you are ready.

When you are ready and don't go, that is almost as bad as going before you are ready.

Eight Essential Criteria For Success

ELEMENT ⬇ STATUS ⮕	1	2	3	4	5	6	7	8	9
A. SPENDING PLAN	☐	☐	☐	☐	☐	☐	☐	☐	☐
	in committee			Board approval			congregational approvals		
B. FUND-RAISING PLAN	☐	☐	☐	☐	☐	☐			
	study report			Board or committee approval			☐	☐	☐
C. RESOLUTION	☐	☐	☐	☐	☐	☐	☐	☐	☐
	CDC draft			committee signs			Board signs		
D. CASE STATEMENT	☐	☐	☐	☐	☐	☐	☐	☐	☐
	first draft (CDC or other)			final draft			circulated to leaders		
E. PROSPECT LIST	☐	☐	☐	☐	☐	☐	☐	☐	☐
	compiled			posted			evaluated		
F. LEADERS	☐	☐	☐	☐	☐	☐	☐	☐	☐
	identified			qualified			invited		
G. ORGANIZATION	☐	☐	☐	☐	☐	☐	☐	☐	☐
	diagram & table			campaign committee			capital gifts		
H. BUDGET	☐	☐	☐	☐	☐	☐	☐	☐	☐
	CDC draft			committee approval			treasurer enlisted		

1 ☐ started   2 ☐ in process   3 ☐ completed

16 WAYS TO INCREASE GIVING

Some immediate, practical help for your church.

1. ESTABLISH A YEAR-ROUND STEWARDSHIP COMMITTEE. There is more to stewardship development than the annual every-member canvass. Stewardship learning and performance flourish in an atmosphere of quiet but constant cultivation.

2. SET HIGHER GOALS. The giving potential of the congregation is far beyond its accustomed level. Only unprecedented goals produce unprecedented performance.

3. GET BACK TO FIRST CENTURY COMMUNICA-TION. The early Christian churches had no mimeographs, photo-copiers, or printing presses. They prevailed through face-to-face talk; person to person and in small groups.

4. BE A GIVING CHURCH. By its own giving, the church sets its members a compelling example. Church giving off the bottom generates members' giving off the bottom; church giving off the top generates members' giving off the top.

5. RAISE CAPITAL FUNDS SEPARATELY. Except for mission churches and preaching stations, few church mortgages are really necessary. You can raise more building funds in any one year than budget funds. Keep capital funds out of the budget; that is expensive and a drag.

6. GET YOUR BEST AND BIGGEST GIFTS FIRST. Rather than mailing the pledge cards and then calling on those who do not respond, call first on your prospective best and largest gifts. Spend 85 percent of your time where 85 percent of the money will come from—not on the last 15 percent, where very little will happen.

7. WEAR HANDCUFFS. Be pastor to your lay leaders but don't do their work for them. Keep yours hands off the machinery. The question is who is helping whom with whose responsibilities.

8. ORGANIZE YOUR BEST GIVERS. Only good givers make other good givers. Nominal givers make only other nominal givers.

9. TEACH THE HABIT OF WEEKLY PLEDGING.
Presenting one's offering is an essential part of worship.
Sending a quarterly check is no substitute for *bringing* one's
offering to worship service. Send weekly envelopes to *all*
your families.

10. RECOGNIZE AND HONOR GOOD GIVERS.
With the permission of the givers—and *only* then—let the
congregation know about 'some of the fine giving that is
going on around here.' "Let your light so shine..."

11. PROVIDE INDIVIDUAL GUIDELINES. For most
families, "How much should we give" is a wrenching decision. Be prepared to offer specific, helpful suggestions for
individual cases, not just bland generalizations.

**12. PROVIDE FOR INDIVIDUAL CONVERSA-
TIONS.** Counselling about Christian giving should be
highly individualized, confidential, and should take place
in the homes. (But you stay out of this.)

13. ENCOURAGE PERSONAL WITNESS. The most
powerful, effective stewardship-development force within a
congregation is the personal testimony of those who have
recently experienced the Gospel of Good Giving.

14. LET THE CONGREGATION TAKE PRIDE. As
the level of giving in the congregation rises, publicize the
good news and keep it flowing. Let the members take pride
in their corporate achievement.

**15. SEE NEW MEMBERS FOR THEIR PLEDGES
RIGHT AWAY.** The next every-member canvass is too
late.

16. PREACH THE GOSPEL OF GOOD GIVING. It really is better to give than to receive. Honest!

PART TWO

Getting the Details Right

FIVE LEVELS OF
ASPIRATION

YOU CAN RAISE A small capital fund by passing the plate one more time or sending a congregational mailing or two. It is not worthwhile to organize for such modest objectives. At the other extreme, in building a new church or relocating, even a professionally-managed campaign for three-year pledges will not alone suffice because the total requirement is more than the members can give within three years.

In computing the potential of a church or, as they say in gymnastics, "degree of difficulty", we use the established giving habit of the congregation as a base. This is the amount that the members are giving, undesignated, to the annual operating budget. It does not include special appeals, earned income, endowment fund yield, gifts of organizations of the church, or anything other than just plain, direct giving of resident members. Whatever that amount for your church let's call that "the budget" even though that isn't accurate. Now, all goals can be expressed in "times the budget". A professional- managed building fund campaign should raise at least three times the budget.

THE 5 LEVELS
1. Offering
2. Big Gifts (only)
3. Short Pledge-payment Period
4. Full Campaign (150 weeks)
5. Fund Raising Program

Let's start with the most modest. For this you need not organize at all. A simple offering will probably do. To organize and visit in the homes would be like using a sledge hammer to drive a carpet tack. Pledges are not necessary.

Between level 1 (Offering) and level 4 (Campaign) you have two options: reduce the pledge-payment period or the number of home visits for pledges. Use whatever pledge-payment period you think appropriate to the goal. Taking your three-year (36 months) potential as 100 percent, the amount that you can raise, as a percentage of your full potential, looks like this:

Pledge-payment period (months)	Percent of potential
36	100 percent
24	72.5
12	40
6	25

The other alternative, to reduce the number of home visits, should be conducted the opposite of the way you probably conduct your annual every-member canvass. In the conventional EMC, the church mails the pledge cards and then organizes for home visits to those families that do not respond. You thus spend 85 percent of your time and effort collecting the last 15 percent of the money.

Much better is to select carefully that 10 percent or 15 percent of the families who will best repay a personal visit. Then announce what this small number of families has contributed and mail the pledge cards to the balance of the congregation.

An intermediate between a personal visit and a mailed pledge card is a telephone call. A telephone call often is three times as productive as a letter and a home visit can be three times as productive as a telephone call. The statistical problem is that we know that the relative power of the visit increases as the size of the proposed or actual gift increases but we don't know by how much. Obviously, if you seek a million-dollar gift, a letter is useless, a telephone call is inappropriate enough to be ill-received, and only personal conversations will do.

At the top, you have a fund-raising program, which is our name for achieving a goal that cannot be attained through a single campaign. On this level, the most common and probably the best practice is a two-stepper: (1) a campaign for three-year pledges, followed immediately by (2) a campaign for two-year pledges.

An interesting variation on this plan is to use "combined fund" pledges for the second campaign. In this style, the pledge is for the total amount of the families' contribution to the capital fund *and* operating fund. Never, never do this in the first campaign but in the second it is all right.

Following the completion of the two-year pledge-payment period, you can conduct the greatest annual every-member canvass in the history of the church. You have (1) temporarily doubled or even tripled the total amount that the members contribute to the church by securing separate, three-year, building-fund pledges; then you (2) blended the two commitments into a single figure but retained the temporary nature of the pledge by specifying an ending date. Now, (3) you can remove the ending date. Churches have been known to triple their regular budget giving through this five year, three-step process.

Obviously, a fund-raising program requires long-range vision, patience, tenacity, and lots of good, hard work.

30

THE DECISION TO CAMPAIGN

THE CAMPAIGN THAT RAISES only 75 percent of its goals is not the loser. The campaign that never got started is the loser. 75 percent beats 0 percent any time. Sometimes the decision to campaign is difficult to secure, sometimes even impossible. Thorough preparation is always advisable. Before submitting the suggestion of a campaign for official decision, somebody must do these things:

1. COMPREHENSIVE COSTS. Secure rough estimates of *all* that is proposed: land purchase, site improvement, new construction, furniture and fixtures, fees, short-term construction loans, and fund raising. Do not eliminate anything. Do not, for instance, plan to get the costs of furniture after the campaign. Do not fragment the goal in any way.

2. INTEREST COSTS. Calculate the cost of borrowing. This includes selling bonds to the congregation, for that is only borrowing and nothing more. Get a copy of *Comprehensive Mortgage Payment Tables* from your banker or from Financial Publishing Company, 82 Brookline Avenue, Boston, MA 12215, and compute the various possibilities.

3. FUND-RAISING POTENTIAL and costs. Secure an estimate of your fund-raising potential and an estimate of total fund-raising costs (fees and expenses) from a reliable firm of fund-raising consultants*. You will be surprised at how much less it will cost to raise than to borrow the funds you need.

4. A COMMITTEE OF THE BOARD. Place the information you have gathered in the hands of a committee of the Board that is charged with responsibility to make a recommendation to the Board. (Usually, it is even better if the Committee conducts these preliminary investigations but you have to start the ball rolling yourself.)

5. HOME MEETINGS. Take a draft of the *tentatively* approved resolution to conduct the campaign to the congregation through a series of small meetings in the homes of the members. Little sessions of six or eight couples will discuss the plan more intelligently, and come up with more good ideas, than any big congregational meeting.

Following these five steps the Board takes official action.

*For a list of consultants, or more information, write the American Association of Fund-Raising Counsel, 25 West 43rd Street, New York, NY 10036.

Many a pastor has told me, "We don't have to go through all those preliminary steps. The congregation has never voted me down on anything." But if you don't take the time and the trouble to prepare carefully this could be the first time that the congregation has voted you down.

31

A FUND-RAISING POLICY COMMITTEE

I T IS A GOOD idea to have a committee of the Board responsible for the preparations just discussed, rather than for the minister to do them. This can be a standing finance or stewardship committee, but an ad hoc committee selected exclusively for the purpose is even better.

This policy committee, by whatever name, should also recommend to the Board whether you will have a do-it-yourself or a professionally-managed campaign. (If you are really going for your full potential, you had better bring in the pros.) The question, here, is not who will actually raise the funds—the campaign organization will do that. The question is whether the leaders of the campaign organization will plan and self-manage the operation or whether they will hire a firm to do this for them.

The policy committee should also secure an appropriation from the Board for total campaign expenses.

The policy committee is not the fund-raising organization. It selects and secures the Campaign Chair and then retires into the background while the campaign is organized and conducted, emerging only to make a full campaign report to the Board, where-upon it is dismissed with thanks. However, a recent development is to keep this committee in being for the pledge-payment period, to see that the post-campaign program is properly organized and conducted. This involves monitoring pledge payments, seeing that families not visited during the campaign or unable to make up their minds during the campaign period are visited, and that new members are visited upon when they join the church.

32

THE PLEDGE CARD

EXCEPT FOR SMALL PROJECTS, you will want to have your own pledge card printed. Use good printing on good stock. Have the name and address of the family individually entered as shown on the sample (page 108). Don't let any blank pledge cards loose.

Aside from any introductory statement that you might want, the only text you need is: "I will try to give $_____ a week for 150 weeks (assuming that you are using a three-year pledge-payment period) for a total gift of $_____ beginning_____." Also provide space for back credits if you are using them and for the names of other members of the family (other than the signer). The Visitor (solicitor) should also sign the card and date it.

The specimen shown has two tabs. When a member of the campaign organization selects the card, he signs the outside tab and gives it to his Chair, Team Leader or the Campaign Secretary. That tab goes to the campaign office, which always has a record of where every pledge card is. The inside tab provides essential information about the family for the Visitor; this information will vary from campaign to campaign, church to church, and family to family.

When the tabs have been removed, the pledge card is 4″ × 6″.

Avoid loading the 4″ × 6″ main section of the pledge card with anything other than that shown on the specimen. For instance, don't have boxes to check off whether the pledge will be paid weekly, monthly, annually, etc. The pledge should be expressed in only weekly and total amounts. How it will actually be paid is another matter that need not concern the Visitor nor the construction of the pledge card.

Extensive experimentation has shown that the collections experience on "I will try to give" is every bit as good as more formal, binding statements.

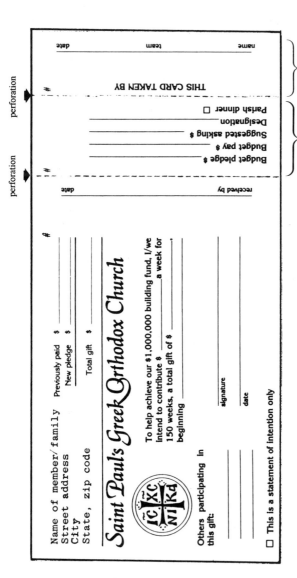

THE PLEDGE CARD

ASSIGNMENT STUB. When a canvasser takes the pledge card, he signs it, and gives it to the Campaign Secretary. 4" x 1".

CANVASSERS INFORMATION STUB. Gives him essential information about the family. 4" x n.

BODY OF THE PLEDGE CARD. It must be 4" x 6", good stock but not fancy. Family name and address should be typed or run on the mailing machine in the upper left corner. The exact form shown here is recommended.

"Previously paid" (upper right) is to credit the family with any previous paid contributions to this same fund.

The # sign in the extreme upper right—and also on the two stubs—is where the alphabetic code # of that family should appear—on all three sections of the card.

"Others participating in this gift" is an optional but nice way for other members of the family to indicate their support of the family pledge.

33

BACK CREDITS

I F YOUR CHURCH has already conducted some fund-raising for the same goal that you now propose, the decent and effective thing to do is to give full credit for all identifiable gifts that have already been made. The natural, human tendency is to wipe the slate clean; to start fresh as though there had been no previous giving. But this is neither fair nor productive.

Interpret and publicize the new campaign as the continuation of a total fund-raising program. Publish the goal as, for instance, "$500,000, of which we already have

$100,000." On each pledge card these three lines should appear:

$_____previously paid
$_____new pledge
$_____TOTAL GIFT

Note that the back credit (the first line) is for the amount previously *paid*. Outstanding amounts pledged but not paid are automatically canceled with the signing of a new pledge.

When there is any question about what a family has previously paid, unquestioningly accept its recollection of the amount.

Admittedly, back credits complicate campaign scoreboarding and gift records. But the extra work is a small price to pay for the powerful benefits-both financial and spiritual-of full recognition and continuity. As one pastor said, "The Lord doesn't care how many decisions you had to make; what does count is your total gift." And you may be certain that that is the way previous givers figure it, no matter how the church does.

BUILDING-FUND-PLUS-BUDGET (BF&B) CAMPAIGNS

I F YOU WANT TO conduct a capital fund campaign at the usual time of your every-member canvass, or if for any reason you want to protect your budget pledging, you can conduct a two-pledge-card campaign. If you do it right, you can increase your budget pledging modestly without decreasing in the slightest the amount raised for the capital fund.

In a BF&B campaign, each family is asked first to sign a budget pledge and *then* a capital-fund pledge. Both pledges can be secured on the same visit but the budget pledge must be signed first. In fact, it is good practice to staple the budget card on top of the building-fund card.

Never, *never*, NEVER use one pledge card for both funds.

Provide space to specify the beginning payment date of the budget pledge but not an ending date. The family indicates only how much a week it will try to give starting when. There is no reason ever to specify an ending date of a budget pledge.

In this two-pledge-card campaign, do not set a budget goal. You will secure a modest increase in budget pledging. But when seeking an important capital fund, don't try simultaneously for a spectacular increase in budget pledging.

If you have not been securing your budget pledges through home visits for the past few years, you will experience a substantial increase in the *number* of budget pledges. You will also increase the percentage of your income that is derived from pledge payments—possibly the most valuable source of income that you can have. But no budget-increase goal, please.

35

ORGANIZATION

A FULL CAMPAIGN, calculated to deliver a personal visit to each member-family in its home, will require a total organization of about 20 percent of the family count. It works out about like this for every 100 families:

100 families
<u>10 Advance Gifts families (10 percent of the total)</u>
90 families, net, in the Campaign Division
18 members in the Campaign Division, themselves

72 families to be visited by the Campaign Division
12 team members required (72 ÷ average of 6)
 2 teams (12 team members ÷ average of 6)

The Campaign Chair secures the pledges of the Team Leaders. The Team Leaders secure the pledges of their Team Members (Visitors). If you require more than six or eight teams, you will have to insert one or more Division Leaders (or Campaign Vice-chairs) between the Campaign Chair and the Team Leaders.

Using this table as a guide, you can easily create a good table or organization for your church. Just don't worry about symmetry and precise arithmetic ratios. A manager (for instance, a Team Leader) can lead from four to eight persons doing identical work. A Visitor will average between five and eight completed assignments (pledges).

	per 100 families	per your family count
Families	100	_____
Advance Gifts (20 percent)	20	_____
Net to Campaign Division (80 percent)	80	_____
Campaign division itself (÷ 5)	18	_____
Net to Campaign Division	72	_____
Team members required (÷ 6)	12	_____
Teams required (÷ 6)	2	_____
Sections required (÷ 6)	0	_____

36

THE TEAM: BUILDING BLOCK OF THE CAMPAIGN ORGANIZATION

YOU WILL NOTE that the campaign organization chart (p. 117) shows (about) eight members of the Advance Gifts Committee and (about) 40 team members in the Campaign Division. Now what is a team?

A team is a group of four to eight visitors or canvassers or solicitors or team members—these names all mean the same thing, a person who makes an exemplary pledge and then selects and visits other families of the church to help them make their pledges.

Members of a team visit their prospects individually for

the most part, but they sit together at team tables at all meetings, they report—and are scoreboarded—as a team, and they help each other in many ways. They often exchange selected pledge cards, or one person "goes with" a fellow team member upon request. They exchange experiences and ideas. They encourage and support each other.

The Team Leader selects his prospective team members, secures their pledges, and is responsible for his team's attendance at report meetings. He also selects the families that he will visit, just as his team members do. Team Leaders are the pivot men in any campaign.

A sample campaign organization chart is on next page.

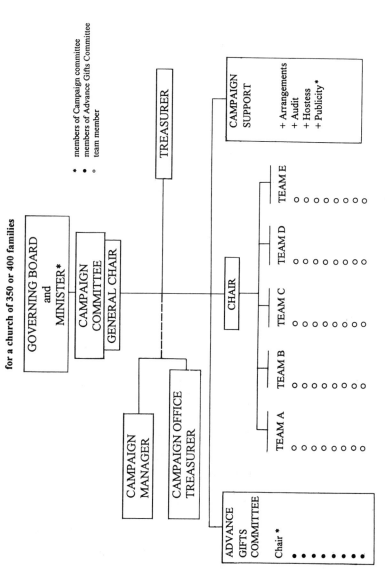

CAMPAIGN ORGANIZATION

for a church of 350 or 400 families

* members of Campaign committee
● members of Advance Gifts Committee
○ team member

GOVERNING BOARD and MINISTER*

CAMPAIGN COMMITTEE
GENERAL CHAIR

CAMPAIGN MANAGER

CAMPAIGN OFFICE TREASURER

ADVANCE GIFTS COMMITTEE

Chair * ● ● ● ● ● ● ● ● ●

TREASURER

CAMPAIGN SUPPORT

+ Arrangements
+ Audit
+ Hostess
+ Publicity*

CHAIR

TEAM A	TEAM B	TEAM C	TEAM D	TEAM E
○○○○○○○○	○○○○○○○○	○○○○○○○○	○○○○○○○○	○○○○○○○○

This specimen shows five teams averaging eight team members each. But variations — such as eight teams averaging five team members each — will not affect performance. This is an actual chart from a real campaign.

117

37

ONLY GOOD GIVERS

THERE IS A GENERAL and there is a special law in fund-raising that are perhaps as important as any whole book ever written on the subject.

The general law: only good givers make other good givers.

The special law: only good givers to this particular project make good givers to this particular project.

Non-givers to this particular project make non-givers to this particular project. Poor givers to this particular project make poor givers to this particular project. Middling givers to this particular project make middling givers to this particular project. Good givers to this project make good givers to this project. Great givers to this project make great givers to this project.

"Good" giving has two dimensions: the size and the generosity of the gift. It is unusual for a member of the campaign organization to bring in a gift larger or more generous than his own. It happens, but not often enough to constitute good fund-raising practice.

Moral: Don't let any middling, poor, or non-givers into the fund-raising organization.

38

THE MINISTER'S ROLE IN FUND RAISING

FUND RAISING IS ESSENTIALLY a lay responsibility. The minister should accept no specific position in the campaign organization. However, the minister is the most important person in the campaign.

As spiritual adviser, he or she should guide, assist, encourage, and support each of the campaign leaders. The minister is not a fund-raiser but his spirit should permeate the entire fund-raising organization.

It is usually best if the minister neither asks anyone to serve in the campaign nor asks anyone for money. Rather, the minister will be asked by various campaign leaders, from time to time, to "go with"—to assist in securing an important agreement to serve or to give.

No member of the church is going to accept a position of campaign leadership without his minister's specific endorsement. Nor will any family make a gift of towering importance to the campaign without discussing it with the minister. But in these all-important conversations, it is usually best if the minister goes with a lay leader.

The minister's own gift is the most important that will be made in the entire campaign. This gift should be made early (but not before the campaign) and should be personally witnessed. A well-established formula is for the minister (or, in larger churches, the ministerial staff) to give 1 percent of the goal.

The minister is, ex-officio, a member of all campaign committees and should attend all that he can, but not chair any of them.

At every important campaign meeting the minister should be the last speaker on the program. After his or her remarks and benediction, adjournment must follow immediately.

39

THE CAMPAIGN CALENDAR

Y OU MUST SET UP a schedule, a calendar for the campaign. But don't worship it. Professional campaign managers publish only tentative calendars. The object of the campaign is to win, not to stay on schedule.

The accompanying table (p. 124) of campaign weeks and the sample calendar (p. 125, 126) can be helpful but should not be followed rigidly. In a campaign for $3 million that I supervised, when I met with the minister about the middle of the campaign period his first question was: "Are we on schedule." I gave him the only possible honest answer:

"No, be we are winning." (The campaign raised $5 million, but not on schedule.)

After a period of preparation, your campaign committee begins its meetings to approve the campaign plan, select leadership, and develop the suggested askings. The Advance Gifts Committee is organized as soon as possible and, as the chart shows, continues right up to the congregational dinner.

The Campaign Division organizes while the Advance Gifts Committee is operating and should, by the time of the Congregational Dinner, have achieved a full and fully-pledged organization.

The pivot point of the calendar is a congregational dinner to which all members are invited (see p. 127). It is best held off the church property. No charge for the dinner. The program that night is to explain the need for the campaign, the goal, and the campaign methods, and to introduce the campaign leaders, announce a few pace-setting pledges and the amount raised to date. There must be no solicitation at the dinner.

Two days after the congregational dinner the campaign officially opens. Thereafter, the Campaign Division holds three report meetings a week — 9:00 p.m. Mondays, Wednesdays, and Fridays — with a final victory report meeting on a Sunday or Monday night. On the specimen calendar, we show an opening dinner for the campaign division, six report meetings over the next two weeks, and a final, victory report meeting, the following Sunday.

You will need a mop-up operation. No campaign can deliver a visit in the home of *every* member-family on schedule. But do not use your full campaign organization for this: set up a cadre of your Team Leaders and a few Visitors who performed well in the campaign, and let them mop-up. This is preferred to extending the meetings of the full campaign organization which, past a certain point, can become boring.

Revise your campaign calendar (see samples, next page) as may be found necessary as the campaign proceeds. Naturally, it is better if you can stay with your original schedule, but it is not vital.

LENGTH OF CAMPAIGN
according to the size of the congregation

Number of member-families	Campaign period (weeks)	# of report meetings
to 80	4	4
to 130	5	5
to 210	6	6
to 880	7	7
to 1,440	9	8
to 2,330	11	9
+ 2,330	12	10

Use this table of campaign length as a guide only. You may require more time for preparation than we have provided here. But be slow to extend the active solicitation (of the Campaign Division) or to increase the number of report meetings.

OCTOBER 199__

EAST HEIGHTS UNITED METHODIST CHURCH

Sunday	Monday	Tuesday	Wednesday	Thursday	Friday	Saturday
September 27 Campaign Manager arrives	September 28 Campaign office opens Interviews	September 29 Interviews B/F Committee Mail Pastoral Letter	September 30 Publicity Chair #1 Evaluations Committee #1 Cong. Dinner invites to Printer	1 Arrangements Chair #1 Evaluations Committee #2	2 Head Hostess #1 Evaluations Committee #3	3 WEEK 1
4 Pulpit announcement General Chair	5	6 Campaign Committee #1 Deadline/select Vice Hostesses	7	8 Team Leader Visitor instructions delivered Select Hostesses	9 A/G Committee #1 Campaign booklet to printer	10 WEEK 2
11 Pulpit announcement A/G Chair Deadline/Hostess selection	12 Section Leaders #1	13 Campaign Committee #2	14 Hostess card selection #1	15 Section Leaders #2	16 A/G Committee #2	17 WEEK 3
18 Pulpit announcement Head Hostess	19 Team Leaders #1 (Arr. Comm.)	20 Campaign Committee #3	21 Hostesses Check-up Mtg. #2 (Arr. Comm.)	22 Team Leaders #2 (Arr. Comm.)	23 A/G Committee #3 Hostess table cards & scoreboards delivered	24 WEEK 4 Attendance cards, prayer cards, campaign booklet, envelopes delivered
25 Pulpit announcement Minister	26 A/G Committee #4 Teams Instructor #1 (Arr. Comm.)	27 Vice Hostesses Check-up Mtg. #3 (Arr. Comm.) Campaign Committee #4	28 CONGREGATIONAL DINNER (Arr. Comm.)	29 Report envelopes & Team table cards delivered	30 OPENING DINNER/DESSERT Teams Organization #2 (Arr. Comm.)	31 WEEK 5

SAMPLE CAMPAIGN CALENDAR
EAST HEIGHTS UNITED METHODIST CHURCH

NOVEMBER 199__

Sunday	Monday	Tuesday	Wednesday	Thursday	Friday	Saturday
1	2	3	4	5	6	7 **WEEK 6**
8 Pulpit announcement	9	10 Campaign Committee #5	11 Report Meeting #2 (Arr. Comm.)	12 A/G Committee #5	13 Report Meeting #3 (Arr. Comm.)	14 **WEEK 7**
15 Pulpit announcement P.O. Chair	16 Report Meeting #4 (Arr. Comm.)	17	18 Report Meeting #5 (Arr. Comm.)	19 Continuation Committee #1	20 Victory Report Mtg. #6 (Arr. Comm.)	21 **WEEK 8**
22 Campaign Manager departs Final Report Pulpit announcement General Chair	23	24	25 Continuation Committee #2	26	27	28
29	30					

CONGREGATIONAL DINNER

If you are going for a maximum goal, you may want to hold a dinnner for the entire congregation a few days before the formal opening of the campaign. Do not have this at the church. Do not charge for the dinner; find one member to pay the whole bill. No outside speakers. Do not take up gifts, pledges, or a collection. Do announce (1) exemplary gifts by name and amount (with the permission of the givers) and (2) the total amount contributed to date, which ought to be at least 40% of the goal. Take up prayer pledges (page 128).

AGENDA

Presiding: Senior campaign chairman

WHEN	WHAT	WHO [1]
6:30	Reception and seating	
7:30	Opening prayer	Pastor
7:32	Dinner	
8:15	Introductions & opening remarks	Presiding chair
8:25	Our church	Well-known member
8:35	Our opportunity	Board chair
8:45	The campaign: goal and methods	Campaign chair
8:55	Early pledges and total amount already raised [2]	Advance Gifts chair
9:05	Introduce campaign organization	Presiding chair
9:15	How to make a pledge	Campaign chair
9:25	Closing remarks and prayer [3]	Pastor
9:35	Adjourn	Pastor

1. Only those who have already made an exemplary pledge and accepted a position in the campaign organization should appear on the program.

2. Announce eight or ten fine pledges (with permission of the givers).

3. As part of his presentation, the Pastor explains the prayer pledge card and asks everyone to sign–as he and his wife now sign their own.

Prayer Pledge

At each evening meal from now until the close of the campaign I shall take my mind from whatever I have been doing and pray that we shall achieve victory in this campaign. This I pledge to do, knowing that the other members of the Church will join me in this prayer each day.

_____

Signature

For some churches this text will suffice. Others will prefer that the Pastor write a prayer that all will use. In the latter case, the card should have two sections, separated by a perforation: the signed pledge to be turned in, and the prayer text to be kept.

40

GUIDELINES TO GIVING

Y OU SEEK NOT EQUAL but proportionate gifts—proportionate to the individual family's financial capability. This takes some doing. Your members need guidance in resolving the all-important question: How much should we give? Most of your families will sincerely struggle with this question. And, in that struggle, they need all the help that the church can give.

The more specific that help—in terms of dollars, not percentages, formulae, or generalities—the better. If you can, have the campaign committee work out presumably equitable dollar-amount suggestions for all families. This is a long and difficult task, and it can never be done to anybody's complete satisfaction, but is the most helpful of all the alternatives.

I have also had very good responses—although not so good as specific dollar amounts—with "one dollar a week for every thousand dollars annual income." In small churches striving mightily to build a proper church plant, or in churches that have already achieved a high level of budget giving, we do frequently go to "two dollars a week for every thousand dollars of annual income."

Strangely, if you suggest that a family give 5 percent of its income, or any other percentage, what you mostly get is an argument: "Before or after taxes? . . ." etc. But the $1 per $1,000 does not produce arguments. That doesn't mean all families will give it, but it does mean that they accept it as a guideline.

Don't use the tithe as a guideline because that is more applicable to budget giving than to capital fund giving. It is interesting to note that the Muslim tithe is on capital rather than income. But that idea is seldom acceptable in Christian churches.

41

DISTRIBUTION OF GIFTS BY SIZE AND NUMBER

YOU HAVE OFTEN HEARD it said that "15 percent of the gifts should produce half of the total goal, and 85 percent the other half." There is a good bit of truth in this cliche but, like most time-honored maxims, it is simplistic.

Professional campaign managers recognize three kinds of churches according to the distribution of assets and income among families:

1. METRO, wherein there is a considerable distance between the financially most-capable families and the

modal families. (Modal means what you have the most of.)

2. COMMUNITY, wherein there is less distance between the most-capable and the modal families.
3. TRACT, wherein there is very little distance between the top and the modal.

The bromide, "50 percent from 15 percent" applies in only a very general way and actually is more applicable to tract churches than to the other two kinds. The three formulae are:

DOLLARS	METRO	COMM.	TRACT
first 25%	1%	3%	5%
second 25%	10	10	10
third 25%	20	20	20
fourth 25%	69	67	65

You can quickly see that the difference among the three kinds of churches is the percentage of the goal that the largest gifts can account for. On the Metro scale, a mere 1 percent of the families can produce 25 percent of the goal. On the tract, it will require 5 percent of the families to produce the first 25 percent of the goal.

In actual practice, there is a fourth type, wherein more than 5 percent of the gifts are required to produce the first 25 percent of the dollars. However, a shared characteristic of churches of this type is that the total giving, or average giving per family, is low.

Where is your church among these four types? Wherever you think it is, move it up one notch. That is, if you think yours is a tract church, it is much more probably a community; if you think it is a community, it is much more probably a metro.

In suggesting guidelines—or, preferably, specific, dollar-amount suggestions for individual families—check yourself (or your committee) to see that the suggested amounts are distributed among the families according to the kind of church that you have. That is, if you are a metro church, the campaign must be prepared to ask 1 percent of the families to give the first 25 percent of the goal.

If all of this strikes you as though we are asking too much of your financially most-capable families, consider: almost nobody ever gives more than they are asked to give. John Rockefeller said that when he was being solicited he always asked the importuner how much he thought that he, Rockefeller, should give; and that it was frequently less than Rockefeller already had in mind.

The amount that the churches of the United Sates and Canada lose each year by asking too little of their financially most capable families certainly runs into the hundreds of millions of dollars, and more probably into the billions—what we call "the uninvited billions".

To ask that a member or family think about giving a certain amount need not be crude, pushing, or high- pressure. In Rockefeller's own phrase, "Perhaps you might be willing to consider..."

42

HOME VISITS: SOLO OR DUET?

THE POPULAR CUSTOM IS to make the home visits in pairs. The origins of this practice are obscure but the results are clear. A member of the duet visit takes more time coordinating schedule with his partner than he does visiting. In the actual conversation in the home, the members of the duet mostly stumble over each other's feet. The advice, guidance, and help that the family needs is seldom provided by two persons simultaneously.

However, a good team will discuss each visiting assignment individually and make individual decisions. The best way to resolve this old, knotty problem is simply to leave it up to the team member who takes the pledge card of a particular family. If he wants help, he will ask another member of his team for it. If he would rather go alone, he will do that. Let nobody on high try to legislate the matter.

The most frequent situation in which two visitors are indicated is when one of the team members knows the family to be visited but his own gift is less than the family should be asked to consider. In that case, he might well ask a larger giver on his team to "go with", because it is difficult to advise anyone to make a larger gift than one has, oneself, given.

But, in almost all cases, one evangelist will do better than two or three or any other number, although exceptions to this rule are often encountered in Advance Gifts.

Perhaps the most crushing observation about the duet system is that it means you must either build a campaign organization twice the size that the professionals use, or the average team member will have to make twice as many visits.

43

REPORTING CAMPAIGN PROGRESS

T HE CONVENTIONAL THERMOMETER THAT shows what percentage of the goal has been achieved to date is not only useless, it can be downright misleading. Consider that if, in a campaign for $500,000, you had planned that the ten largest gifts would account for $200,000 but, in fact, they disappointingly accounted for only $100,000.

Your conventional thermometer would show that 5 percent of your families had contributed 20 percent of the goal —and there would be great rejoicing and even dancing in the streets—whereas you have probably lost your campaign. Those families should have accounted for 40 percent of the goal, not 20 percent and there is no way you can make up the difference.

The best way to report progress visually is on what we call a hollow-bar chart. The hollow bars show the size and number of the gifts that you seek. As gifts are secured, you fill in the bars. About one-third of the way through a campaign, with two-thirds of the goal reported, your successor to the old thermometer might look like this gift table (see p. 138).

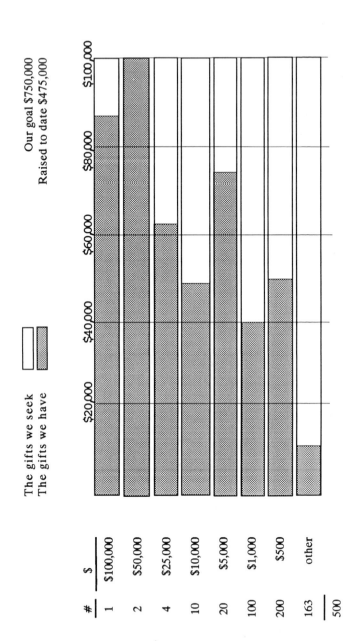

GIFT TABLE

The gifts we seek
The gifts we have

Our goal $750,000
Raised to date $475,000

#	$
1	$100,000
2	$50,000
4	$25,000
10	$10,000
20	$5,000
100	$1,000
200	$500
163	other
500	

POST-CAMPAIGN:
A POSSIBLE 30
PERCENT SWING

W HAT PERCENTAGE OF THE total amount shown on the
campaign scoreboard at the victory report meeting
will actually be collected? If you follow the common practice of doing very little about it, the probability is about 85
percent or maybe 90 percent. But if you will take some
pains, the actual amount collected can be 115 percent of the
scoreboard total. That is a swing of as much as 30 percent.
That is worth quite a bit of effort, isn't it?

To insure good payments on amounts pledged, set up a
monitoring committee. This group meets monthly and re-

views all delinquent pledges. It finds what the problem is in each individual case, then decides what to do about it, and then does it or sees that it is done.

The monitoring committee must have authority to reduce or even cancel a pledge, or to set up a new schedule of delayed or reduced payments. Families experiencing temporary financial hardships are often encouraged, by such a committee, to reduce or suspend payments for a while and extend their payment schedule beyond the formal 150-week (or whatever) period.

To increase the total amount pledged, another group visits the new families as they join the church and secures their pledges for the remainder of the pledge-payment period. For instance, a family joining one year following the campaign will be invited to pledge for 100 weeks.

This committee is also alert for opportunities to secure pledges from those who were not contacted in the campaign or could not make up their minds how much to give, or who asked to be seen later.

The church should send quarterly reminder notices of the status of individual pledge payments.

45

NON-MONEY GIFTS

W HEN WE TALK OF fund-raising we think of money-raising—too often. What part of a family's assets or estate consists of cash in the bank? Very little. In 1982, somewhere between 75 and 100 gifts of $1 million or more were made to nonprofit organizations. How many of these were cash gifts? My personal estimate: none.

Most estates consist of homes, other real estate, personal property, stocks, bonds and notes. All of these can be given to the church just as well as cash. In fact, often the tax advantages to the givers can far exceed the advantages of cash.

Your church should have a foundation; that is, a nonprofit organization controlled by, but separate from, the church. This organization can be a recipient of both cash and non-cash gifts, especially non-cash, and especially bequests.

In setting up your church's own foundation, secure competent legal advice. Select and secure as trustees persons known for their experience and success in handling very, very large amounts of money. Their financial and fiduciary reputations will encourage gifts and bequests.

One warning: do not allow the foundation to subsidize the annual operating budget. Budget subsidies of any kind diminish the regular contributions of living, resident members.

46

REASONS VERSUS EXCUSES

I N ALL FUND-RAISING ORGANIZATION, select the best-qualified person for an individual position of leadership. Do not have alternatives because you won't need them.

In all solicitation, invite the family to consider giving a gift of a specific amount. Do not suggest a range of amounts or even a formula if you can possibly avoid it. Do not be concerned with the consequences of a refusal, or of a smaller gift than you anticipate, because neither one is going to happen.

When the person asked to serve knows that the right position has been selected for him—when he understands that he is the best-qualified person in the congregation for that position—he will serve.

When the family knows that it is asked to give an amount that is right for it and for the campaign, the family will give that amount.

Occasionally you will encounter a reason for not serving or not giving that you had not anticipated because there is something about the person or family that you did not know. There are, now and then, reasons for refusals. But nine times out of ten that you experience a negative response, what is given as a reason is not a reason at all—it is an excuse. There is a world of difference.

A legitimate reason must be accepted. ("I cannot serve as Chair because I am leaving tomorrow morning on an around the world trip and will be gone for four months." or "We cannot give what you ask because we are bankrupt and asking for protection under chapter 11.") But excuses are something different.

The important thing is not to answer excuses. Don't hear them. Pay no attention to them. If you do, you are sunk.

An excuse cannot be answered because it is not valid, it is not real. The person who will offer excuses can think them up faster than you can respond to them. When you try to answer an excuse you are playing the other person's ball game, and you have already lost the game.

Sam called on Al for his pledge to the building fund. Al refused to give. "Why?" asked Sam.

Al looked annoyed. "Well, if you must know, I don't like the pastor."

"What don't you like about the pastor?" asked an astonished Sam.

Al looked even more uncomfortable and finally blurted out, "He wears those yellow shoes."

"Now Al", said Sam, "What in the world does the pastor wearing yellow shoes have to do with your giving to the building fund?"

Now Al was downright angry. "Sam", he spluttered, "you know as well as I do that when you're not going to give, one excuse is as good as another."

And you know, he was right.

THE 11 CARDINAL POINTS (I think)

1. SET HIGH GOALS. The distinction between amateurs and professionals is nowhere made so clearly evident as in the setting of goals. Pedestrian common sense says, "Play it safe, set a low goal." But you and I know that is wrong. Nothing is more difficult than to manage a campaign that everybody knows can't fail because it's easy. Such a campaign receives only low attention or effort from anybody. It keeps on schedule and fails on schedule. If the church is fortunate, finally somebody goes out and gets the unpledged balance from one˙ giver.

2. PLAN THOROUGHLY. When Admiral Byrd came back from man's first flight over the south pole, the reporters clamored, and the first of them to be recognized blurted out, "Tell us of your adventures." The Admiral responded thoughtfully: "We didn't have any. This trip was well planned and prepared. If it hadn't been, we would have had some adventures."

3. USE ONLY BEST-QUALIFIED LEADERS. The amateur complicates this point, but to the true pro it is simple: use as campaign leaders only those who make the biggest and best gifts to the project. If torn between biggest and best, choose biggest. Just don't complicate the subject. The amateur thinks our society is becoming financially equalitarian. The pro knows better.

4. GET THE BIG GIFTS FIRST. The more skilled the campaign manager, the larger the percentage of the total amount raised will be produced from the few biggest gifts. The amateur campaign manager just doesn't understand the way disposable wealth and income are distributed in North America.

5. RELY ON ORGANIZATION, NOT PROMOTION. The neophyte manager will flood the congregation with bulletins, letters and printed materials. But promotion does not raise big money. I stole away 2:00 a.m. at the end of my first campaign to dump my undistributed printed and mimeographed (yes, it was that long ago) materials. My teacher's one boast was that at that point he could put all such in one small wastepaper basket.

6. CREATE A COMMITTED ORGANIZATION. The only church fund-raising organization that is worth its salt is composed exclusively of very good givers *to this project*. Forget all other considerations; they are irrelevant.

7. SEEK PLEDGES IN THE HOMES. The amateur will take up the pledges of the assembled Visitors at meetings. This is one of the best ways to make certain that the manager will never enjoy the good life.

8. USE SUGGESTED ASKINGS. Not one out of a hundred—maybe one of out of a thousand—amateur campaigns will use suggested askings. Not one out of a hundred—perhaps a thousand-campaigns managed by a real pro will fail to use suggested askings. This is a watershed issue, with nobody balanced on the knife-edge top.

9. SEEK 100 PERCENT ATTENDANCE AT REPORT MEETINGS. The morale of the fund-raising organization is generated and sustained at meetings. To expect the individual visitor to sally forth and visit five or ten families productively all on his/her own is naive. The real pro provides for five to eight report meetings and expends considerable time and energy in promoting 100 percent attendance. Campaign organizations that do not frequently assemble to report run downhill fast; they just fizzle out.

10. STAY OFF-STAGE. Campaign managers should work *through* volunteer leaders and workers. My motto is, "If you want a thing done right, don't do it yourself." Stay in the background; off-stage. Neither seek nor accept applause. Campaign managers are paid, and that pay is their reward. It is the volunteers—those who labor only for love of the cause—they are the fund-raisers. We are not fund-raisers. We are fund-raising campaign managers—only that and that is enough. Any who seek personal recognition would be well-advised to seek other employment—to get into some other line of work.

11. TEACH THE GOSPEL OF GOOD GIVING. The level of the motive that propels your campaign leaders has much to do with the level of success that you will experience. Put the campaign on the level of the good news— the gospel that it really *is* better to give than to receive; that the giver really *is* the principal beneficiary of the gift.

The amateur campaign manager predicates everything on the need of the church to receive. The true professional includes the need of the church in the goal but puts even greater emphasis on the need of the person—the family—to give. For to give is to live, and to live is to love, and to love is to give, and to give is to love. There is no other way truly to live. Giving as a duty is a drag.